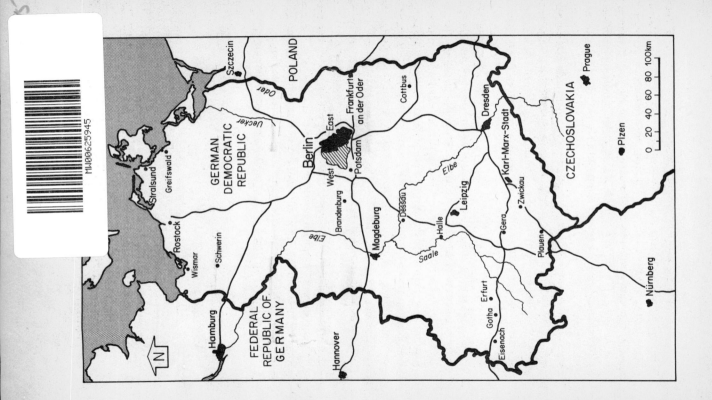

THE UNLOVED COUNTRY

A Portrait of East Germany Today

MICHAEL SIMMONS

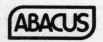

For Stephen and Alastair

AN ABACUS BOOK

First published in Great Britain 1989
in Abacus by Sphere Books Ltd

Printed and bound in Great Britain by
Richard Clay Ltd, Bungay Suffolk

ISBN 03491 01086

Sphere Books Ltd
A Division of
Macdonald & Co. (Publishers) Ltd
66/73 Shoe Lane, London EC4P 4AB
A member of Maxwell Pergamon Publishing Corporation plc

Contents

Acknowledgements

Acknowledgements are due to many people, East and West, who helped me enormously with ideas and materials. The list of names would be very long. It would embarrass some of their owners — so none will be given.

However, I would particularly like to thank the editors of *The Guardian* for letting me use material from the paper, as well as Nicholas Dallman, John Gittings, Joni Lovenduski, Geoffrey Rider, John Röhl and one Well-Placed Diplomat who read some or all of the manuscript with patience and then offered good advice. I would also like to thank my wife, Angela, for bearing with me during days and nights of enforced seclusion; Margit Hosseini for help in research; Heather Dimbleby for good-naturedly typing and re-typing it all; and Julian Evans and Tessa Sayle for making the hard slog of book-writing so enjoyable.

Introduction

Our GDR is the work of millions, of generations, of mothers and daughters, of fathers and sons and grandchildren. The product of the people belongs to the people. Here everyone can say with complete justification: I have helped to build this. This state is a part of me and is the work of my ideas and my hands.

Egon Krenz, East German Politburo member on 2 March 1984

It used to take ten or fifteen years to get an East German car with a small East German engine. Now it is going to take even longer to get the same car with a Volkswagen engine. So, what have we achieved ? . . . .

Senior GDR civil servant and Party member, in conversation, early 1989

The German Democratic Republic, which I have here intermittently called East Germany, has been in its time the most maligned, most disparaged and most misunderstood state in Europe. The title of this book has been borrowed from a West German commentator who said as much about himself and his attitudes as he did about the GDR when he described it as 'the unloved country'. This country, he declared, is 'the victim of an historical mistake'.

Other East Europeans have been similarly dismissive. 'The GDR?' asked a Polish friend, rather askance, as we drank tasteless coffee one rainy day in Warsaw. 'It is nothing. It is warmed and fed by its brothers to the West and it is kept in order by its brothers to the East.'

But more than sixteen million people live there, and these people are Germans — Europeans — who live close to the heart and the inheritance of 'central Europe'. And like their West German counterparts, they claim a descendance from a number of great and good Germans who did much for the cultural and political development of Europe.

East Germany grew awkwardly out of the ashes and the humiliation which followed the Second World War and the achievement has been, by any standards, impressive. A deprived childhood led to a hypersensitive adolescence, with a desperate search for a recognition that was more than diplomatic, and thence to an uncertain prime of life.

Now, with the coming of Mikhail Gorbachev, 'the Soviet bloc' has effectively disintegrated. He has preached reform but has stipulated nothing. He has also authorised each 'Socialist' country to make and follow its own way to Communism, and there are as many 'ways' forward as there are members of the Warsaw Pact. The Pact, incidentally, remains, along with the notional 'threat' from the West, which many see as the only unifying factor among the erstwhile bloc members.

East Germany's leading figures, unlike their West German counterparts, have often shown their war scars and talked of their wartime experience with purpose and pride. The personal trauma of the war made their cause different from the cause of the leaders of, for instance, Czechoslovakia, Hungary or Poland. These, and others, have warned against the deadly peril of (West German) revanchism, but not with the same firsthand knowledge or the same mistrust as the East Germans. In this significant respect, East Germans are of a different make-up and are differently motivated from all other East Europeans.

This is not to suggest that the GDR is merely an 'excuse' for a country rather than a country in its own right. Plenty of other countries in the twentieth century have had their boundaries determined for them and their leaders thrust upon them. Not all have progressed, as the GDR has progressed, to establish their identity beyond doubt, to treat and be treated as an equal on the international stage, and to argue on equal terms about political tactics and political strategy with the hand (in this case, the Soviet Union) which delivered them less than half a century before.

Some East Germans claim that their mission since the founding of the East German state in 1949 has been to complete what was started, and only half-finished, in the attempted revolution of 1918-1919. Now, to keep the revolution alive, the East German leadership has come to invoke what is sometimes called 'GDR nationalism', praising 'Socialism in GDR colours'. There is a fierce pride, and as much ferocity sometimes as pride in the emphasis on the letters DDR (Deutsche Demokratische Republik), and there is no doubt or uncertainty in this sort of vision. But it is a vision which suggests fallibility as well as integrity. 'The dialectic of continuity and renewal,' Günter Mittag, a Politburo member, told a meeting in Leipzig in the spring of 1989, 'means that we will resolutely pursue this policy [of Erich Honecker] — and this will be so up to the year 2000 and beyond because without doubt it is an indispensable part of Socialism.'

In the week that he spoke these words, the Hungarian leadership announced its plans for a constitutionally enshrined multiparty system, and the Polish authorities gave details of a new electoral deal by which anyone in the country, given the required support, could contest a seat in the new Upper House of the Polish Parliament. The course being pursued by the GDR, in other words, is looking increasingly lonely as well as resolute. A whiff of anachronism in the ideological air has been unavoidable.

There have always been uncertainties in the GDR about how to relate to the mighty Soviet Union. At the end of the war, it was declared by Germany's Communists that it would be wrong to impose 'the Soviet system' on Germany. Not many years later, the slogan went up 'Learn from the Soviet Union', and now, in spite of deliberately contrived differences of attitude in some basic areas, the East German leader Erich Honecker still speaks of the Soviet Union as 'our closest ally'.

He knows the GDR was not born as a result of Stalin, or anyone else, snapping their fingers, and one of the more intriguing 'ifs' of twentieth-century European history must centre on what would have happened in Germany if Hitler had not taken over. The

Germans, after all, had a formidable Communist Party at the time and many were in favour of seizing power.

At the bleak Friedrichstrasse crossing-point in Berlin, you soon realise that the process of entering the GDR is not like entering any other East European country. You seem to be going into a high-walled institution, as if to commune with a closed order which has its own rituals and regulations. Visa officials, money changers, passport and customs controllers seem coldly serious and do nothing to diminish this impression. This may be 'the road to Communism', but the disincentives to the curious traveller are many.

Once inside, the environment is extraordinary. You are confronted with a society which owes its origins to the thinking of some nineteenth-century Germans, long dead, but which has been wrenched through the mill of mid-twentieth century European history and now finds itself enmeshed in late twentieth-century culture. It is a society where conformity is required and where — however much the inhabitants may mutter and curse and laugh among themselves — the rules remain sacrosanct.

In the pages that follow I have attempted, as a journalist rather than an historian, to explore the GDR and to 'open up' some of those avenues which, for one reason or another, have been closed. It is a sort of traveller's guide for the traveller who wonders why the GDR behaves and thinks the way it does, and who wonders by what paths the country reached its present beguiling situation, right on the front line of the Warsaw Pact.

I have rather wilfully experimented in the process of exploring. I have offered what I hope may be tantalising glimpses of what some of the towns and cities have to offer; I have tried to breathe a little life into the legends of Marx and Engels and their contemporaries; and I have tried to give some substance to how the country works. During visits to East and West Europe, I have frequently been reminded over the years that, more than anything, the GDR needs as a matter of some urgency *to be explained*.

As the narrative will indicate, I have some good friends in East Germany. A number, unfortunately, may fall away as they read these pages. I think and hope others will understand what I have tried to do, in familiarising Western readers with their environment. Nothing malicious has been intended, and, if some reservations have been expressed, I can only say I would have had at least as many reservations if I had been writing about contemporary Britain in the same way.

PART ONE

A Search for Roots

First Excursion: A Remote Autobahn

The autobahn which Hitler had built from East to West across the southern flank of the GDR (though of course he never anticipated any dismemberment of the Reich) is cracked in places and very much under-used. Hurtling along it at an illegal speed, heading towards a West German frontier that almost nobody ever crosses, has an eeriness that is difficult to describe. And when heavy, almost suffocating snow starts to fall, as it did the last time I travelled it, the effect can be faintly sinister.

The route cuts across a district which outside East Germany is not well known. This is a pity. Not only is it very attractive in places, but decisive moments in German history, and therefore European history as well, were enacted here. Personalities who had vital roles in that history lived and performed here as well. From east of Dresden across to Eisenach, there are place names which would make anyone with more than a passing curiosity about Germany's political inheritance sit up and take notice. The ghosts that haunt the landscape have, in many instances, household names.

But the East German authorities, and especially their very efficient security services, take a stiff view of history and especially of amateurs in that field. Their own breed tend to be heavily qualified, highly respected members of the Academy of Sciences. When the amateur is a journalist with a Western newspaper in town to report the Leipzig Trade Fair, the stiffness can be unyielding. Spontaneity and enthusiasm, which are natural gas to most amateurs, are treated with reserve by GDR officials.

Leipzig lies about halfway along Autobahn 63 and an hour's

drive to the north of it. The search for the roots of Communism in Germany starts here.

Leipzig is a dour, self-regarding city, an earnest mixture of the Gewandhaus Orchestra and international trade fairs, of refined chamber music and heavy-duty earthmovers. But it is also a place where revolutionaries and supposed revolutionaries took refuge in the last century, when the anti-socialist Bismarck and the Prussian police were on the rampage for anything remotely 'subversive' to the stability of the Kingdom or, later, the new German Reich. Saxony, of which Leipzig is a part, was always more radical than other parts of Germany.

It is, officialdom notwithstanding, less officious than East Berlin. In Leipzig, you have the feeling that people have a job to do, a real job, not something in the bureaucracy or an institute of the Academy of Sciences or an ill-defined service industry. In Leipzig, the fair's the thing — one of the biggest in the world — where the world, if it cares enough, can twice a year come and inspect what Socialism-in-practice has achieved in terms of hardware and technology. It is, in other words, a place where non-Socialists can legitimately try to reassure themselves that in the economic sphere, at least, the Soviet threat is not what it has been cracked up to be.

Thousands of exhibitors from scores of countries converge here to pore over and talk about machine tools and measuring instruments, licences and know-how, automation and efficiency. A combination of astute business interests and inbred attitudes, in East-West relations, tinged with suspicion, means that a lot of them are looking over their shoulder as they do so.

Almost half the exhibitors, as well as the huge number of officials who run the fair, are from the German Democratic Republic itself. A country with a population of just over sixteen million manages at the spring event, for instance, to produce several thousand exhibition stands, staffed as a matter of course by earnest young technocrats in sombre suit — or dress — who will anxiously explain abstruse minutiae.

Shoring up this routine is the interest of 'the people'. It is essentially 'for the people' that Leipzig turns itself into an industrial fairground, that East German officials strain every muscle to please sceptical Western journalists, that the alliance with the very different Soviet Union and the wayward Warsaw Pact is maintained, that Karl Marx and Friedrich Engels persevered in an alien land to produce the ultimate ideological recipe. These pages will be in part an attempt to explain the origins and growth of this particular interest, sometimes by looking at places where it was fostered, sometimes at the personalities who took part in the fostering.

My *Travel Guide to the GDR*, published in Dresden, is as political a document as any produced by authorised printers. 'The GDR,' it states at the outset, 'is a socialist state in which the working class wields power in close alliance with the class of co-operative farmers, the socialist intelligentsia and the other strata of the working population.'

This is the sort of sentence that East German schoolchildren, often stifling a yawn, can recite at the drop of a hat. It is also, though few will admit it, a sentence at which many of the same children's parents would expostulate, give a big grin and say: 'Well, you know how it is . . . .'

The interest of the people, or rather those who have thought and fought on the people's behalf, is made clear throughout the fair. For this reason, the enterprises of Karl-Marx-Stadt, known until 1953 as Chemnitz, are well represented. So is the Wilhelm Pieck cable works, the Friedrich Ebert apparatus plant, and so on. Beyond the purlieus of the fair, it is implicit in other ways. Small street stalls sell cheap plastic things, gaudy socks and T-shirts not always available at other times of the year. Crowds, bussed in from other parts of the country, fill the streets. In a huge multi-storey building devoted entirely to books, there is great interest in the printed works of Mikhail Gorbachev. In some East German minds, these amount almost to subversive writing.

Like every other community in East Germany, Leipzig cherishes its past. The history of the GDR started after the Second World War, but almost any account of life pre-1945 is devoured with great enthusiasm. For the same reason, palaces and churches, stock exchanges and meeting places of the elite, even whole streets and squares which were once characterised by poverty and over-crowding, are painstakingly restored.

Leipzig started life at the foot of a castle. Its early economy was boosted by the discovery of silver in nearby hills. Commerce, in other words profit-making and exploitation, was soon close to its heart, though a happy balance was provided by the oldest university on East German soil and the development of music patronage and performance.

Today it is a busy city of nearly 600,000 people, and the noise and crowds mean that it's not all that pleasant to wander round. This fact, and the damage inflicted in the last months of the Second World War, mean that, once you have digested the more obvious restoration work, you have to seek out what you want to see. But there is a beautifully decorated Old Town Hall, started in the sixteenth century, and just across the Market Square is the former Stock Exchange, gutted by bombs during the war but meticulously rebuilt by the Communists. Then there is the so-called King's House, also rebuilt, where it is said Peter the Great stopped over on his way to Holland. There are, too, tell-tale gaps between buildings which have never been properly filled since they were created by British or American bombers or Soviet shell-fire. Their presence is a demonstration of why 'atmosphere' is so often missing in old East German towns and cities. Planners cannot be blamed for everything.

Among its architectural oddities, Leipzig has an incongruous, monumental railway station, built in early twentieth-century Gothic and one of the biggest in Europe. They say it had one grand entrance for the ruling nobility (of the Kaiser's time) and one for the rest of us. Outside there is a taxi rank which draws long queues but not very many taxis. Here, once again, there is one law for the rich — in this case, the gullible Westerner — and one law for the driver's friends.

Leipzig has many new buildings, some the pride of the current regime, some already looking distinctly tatty. One that remains impressive, if heavy and ponderous, is the relatively new home of the Gewandhaus Orchestra, all sculptured concrete and glass. Some of the less impressive structures belong to the university. Goethe, who was a student in Leipzig, described the city as 'Little Paris' — but that was two hundred years ago.

It was an unexpected surprise when my official companion on one visit to Leipzig suddenly said to me: 'I think you should see how poor people live in my country.' A young and obviously ambitious member of the ruling Socialist Unity Party (the SED), he knew as well as I did that this was a departure from the self-esteem, and occasional arrogance, which still tends to qualify everything official East Germans say and do.

We went to a crumbling tenement-type building and to the battered front door of a one-room flat, where an old woman, a widow, hobbled with the aid of a stick to greet us. She had washed and ironed my companion's clothes when he was a student, and was now wearing a dull cotton dress. There was an unmade single bed at the dark end of the room, which was lit by a single, shadeless bulb. The furniture consisted mainly of a table, a hand-operated sewing machine on top of it, and two kitchen chairs. The carpet was threadbare, and the plaster was broken at several points on the undecorated walls. It was comfortless, dank and depressing. She lived now on her sewing.

Perhaps she would have been a casualty in any society. Perhaps her answer, when I asked her the difference between life under the Nazis and life now, was not all that revealing. Shrugging as she showed me the palms of her hands, she replied: 'Not very much.'

From Leipzig I bent the rules to be taken, in the snow-storm and along the remote autobahn, to Wartburg and its castle. Monika, my interpreter, was on my side, knowing I had come not only to write about the fair for a newspaper but also to seek out what I rather pompously called the roots of German Communism. We had been obliged to deal with several hours of hassle from officialdom, simply because the stamp in my passport insisted that I was confined to the city for the duration of my stay. Eventually, against both our predictions, the passport was altered.

At seven a.m. on this bleak morning Horst, a driver who was the friend of a friend, turned up, and the three of us were Wartburg-bound.

It was as well to make the journey in winter, Monika told me, Wartburg's castle is the best known in the GDR. In fine weather it swarms with visitors.

Associations with specific events that have happened here over the last eight hundred years or more have always been enough to stir even the most hardened German's blood. Built high on a crag above the tree-line of the adjoining Thuringian Forest, and very close to East Germany's frontier with the Federal Republic, it was on the day I chose to see it barely visible in the swirling snow. Wagner's liking for the place was understandable.

We drove up through the trees to what appeared to be a deserted fortress complex. It wasn't deserted. Within seconds, an officious official appeared and ordered Horst to take his vehicle back 300 yards down the road. As we awaited Horst's return, hugging ourselves and stamping our feet to keep warm, we persuaded another official, muttering and grudging, to open up the room where Martin Luther, one of Germany's greatest dissidents, was incarcerated and translated the New Testament. After all, Monika told him, I was a visitor from Britain, and I had come all this way in these conditions . . . .

The room was in an outbuilding of the castle, all bare stone and scrubbed wooden walls, bereft of furniture and decoration except a desk (*the* desk?) and three small pictures of the man himself. It was very austere, which Luther might not have minded. It was also clinically clean and about as moving an experience as a dentist's waiting room.

I suggested to Monika that this fusing of the austere and the sanitised was somehow a hallmark of East German attitudes, and especially attitudes to pre-GDR history.

Monika, well chosen for her task and very self-contained, pouted just a little and said, 'Well, if you say so.'

We left it at that.

I bought a Luther post-card at the souvenir stall. Then we went down along the cobbled passageway to the restaurant for a cup of coffee. This time it was the waiter who was officious, barring our way and saying we could only enter his territory if we first removed our anoraks and left them at the room provided.

Once inside, he remained surly, and erect and somehow Prussian, when he took our modest orders. Even Monika was put out, so she changed the subject. 'Did you know,' she asked me, 'that Goethe came here, and that Liszt conducted here and that Wagner set parts of *Tannhäuser* here?'

We left the castle and drove down into Eisenach, a town of just over 50,000 people, where Soviet occupiers took a special interest at the end of the war. Much smaller then, it was a community where political awareness and commitment were by no means all they could have been. There were also the remains of a factory where small motor cars could be manufactured. Small was interesting to the Russians because bigger would have had military overtones and possibilities. Today the ubiquitous, boxy, underpowered Wartburg car is an undoubted commercial asset. It is also an embarrassment to thousands of middle-class East Germans with big-car aspirations.

Eisenach has its share of history, and streets of medieval half-timbered houses. Luther lived here for a few years and it was here that the peasants' uprising of the 1520s had one of its main centres. The great preacher started out as an opponent of the local aristocracy but then sided, in the cause of peace, with those who wanted the uprising suppressed. Today's East Germans see things differently. Martin Luther, says a little book about Eisenach, was 'the reformer and spiritual pioneer of the first bourgeois revolution in Germany'.

In the aftermath of the snowstorm there was a cold mid-March moisture in the air, and the town looked dirty. It was not an auspicious time for sight-seeing. But, like Leipzig, Eisenach has other attractions. The Bachs lived here, and Johann Sebastian was born here in 1685. There is now a Bach museum. Opera came to Eisenach in 1821, when Mozart's *Die Entführung aus dem Serail* was performed at the Golden Lion, an out-of-town inn on the Nuremberg Road. Perhaps incongruously, it was at the Golden Lion later that I was to find some of the roots I was looking for.

Driving back towards Leipzig, skirting along the northern edge of the beckoning hills and the Thuringian Forest, we came after half an hour across the plain to the town of Gotha. Gotha is older and slightly larger, and much more picturesque, than Eisenach. The main market square sweeps down in a gentle slope from a small baroque terrace, with neatly proportioned part-timbered houses on either side, to a sixteenth-century town hall at the bottom.

It has a neatness and compactness that Eisenach lacks and, at the time that I visited it, a certain quietness. Nothing much seems to be happening there. Then I noticed that a large proportion of the people moving about the town centre were in Soviet uniform. Gotha is a garrison town: according to West European diplomats I spoke to later in Berlin, it was progress that the Russians were to be seen out and about in this way (even though they went about silently and in twos). Before Gorbachev's arrival in power in the mid-1980s, these diplomats said, the Russians didn't venture out of barracks at all.

From the historical point of view, the quietness of Gotha is deceptive. Here too I found roots, for it was here that the German working class reached an important turning point, a development which was a cause of no little irritation to 'the two old men' who were then constrained to live in London — Karl Marx and Friedrich Engels.

But Monika, it transpired over a glass of lemon tea, knew little of Marx's critique of the 'Gotha programme', and Horst even less. As it was getting dark, we decided to head back for Leipzig.

There are two other towns in this corner of East Germany which provide vital pieces to the jigsaw of the history of Communism in Germany. Three, if one also includes Jena, where the young Karl Marx was awarded a doctorate by the local university for a thesis on late Greek philosophy. A bust of the man on the Goethe-Allee, by the university, depicts him as heavy-jowled and approximately forty years older than he was when, in absentia, the doctorate was awarded.

The other two towns are Weimar and Erfurt. In terms of cultural history, Weimar has to be the jewel in Germany's crown, a town where, under the patronage of the local nobility, Goethe, Schiller and other men of letters were pre-eminent. Earlier it had been the home of the painter Cranach, and then of Bach who became organist here and a member of the Court orchestra. Germany's first opera house was in Weimar. And so on.

It is a gentle town, extraordinarily well-kept and a joy to anyone who has the time to savour it. I strolled round one summer afternoon and evening after a morning of heavy rain and had the place, melancholy and delightful at the same time, almost completely to myself. I went without a map, which made it all the more pleasing when I discovered that the park by the River Ilm in which I walked was designed by Goethe himself, and that the nicely proportioned little house in that park was where he had lived during his first years in the town.

Then the guide book brought me down to earth. 'In 1919,' it said, 'the newly elected National Assembly met here, far away from the centres of the working class movement and the revolution, to adopt the constitution of the bourgeois state known as the Weimar Republic. This constitution in later years made it possible for fascism to come to power in Germany by legal means. And it was the fascists who erected one of the biggest concentration camps in the vicinity of the town, at Buchenwald.'

Midway between Jena and Weimar comes the unique experience of Erfurt: one of that handful of towns and cities in central Europe which seems to vibrate with history, where, even in the late twentieth century, something in the air 'gets through' and excites the visitor into thoughts and echoes of an eventful past. In the big league, Prague, though still overlaid by its occlusive post-1968 heaviness, obviously has it. Vienna, for all its well-to-do smugness, cannot shake it off, and neither, despite its innate weariness, can the Polish city of Krakow. But in a specifically German context Erfurt has this 'something' at almost every turn.

Being East German, it has succumbed to dismal six- and eight-storey concrete blocks on the outskirts, and in the tidy town centre there is evidence of that peculiar inertia which overtakes East European centres of population that have been zealously policed and centrally planned for too long. Nevertheless, Erfurt remains small enough to grasp and its strength of character, evident in an abundance of medieval architecture, cannot be ignored.

It is a town of many churches, in some parts dominated by them, though the Communist authorities have seen fit to turn the Benedictine monastery into a storeroom. They also make much of the town's admittedly strong humanist traditions and its early links with socialism.

More than most, the centre of Erfurt is a place the visitor should see on foot, a fact which local officialdom has conceded by the creation of a pleasant pedestrianised zone, centred on a shopping precinct called the Anger. The Anger may be rather eighteenth- and nineteenth-century commercial in its ambiance, but a walk away from it, through the much older cobbled market area, where small-scale part-timbered buildings have lost all sense of the perpendicular (and now sell electrical gadgets or political posters) does have its own rewards.

Suddenly, at the end of the old Market Street, the town opens up on to Cathedral Square. This is a cobbled open space the size of several football pitches, and there is a breathtaking view of the twelfth-century cathedral against the sky on the hill opposite, with the triple-spired St Severi Church, only slightly younger, complementing it in a harmony that must have reassured even the town's humanists, and everyone else, ever since they were built.

The overriding impression is that nothing in this part of Erfurt has changed in centuries, except that the rituals of street religion and the bustle of the once entrepreneurial market place have had to give way to political rallies and parades by the Free German Youth, the young Communist movement.

Above all, it is once again the spirit of Martin Luther which haunts the town. Close to the Central Clinic in Lenin Street, there is a fine statue of him, his back turned on the public lavatory. On the stone plinth, there is an unexpected quotation from Psalm 118, 'I shall not die, but live, and declare the works of the Lord.' The man spent several years studying in Erfurt, and the local tricks of imagination, or light, are such that he still seems likely any minute to come barging round the next corner, black cloak flying, holding forth about difficult and highly questionable truths. Justifiably, the East German authorities made much of the 500th anniversary of Luther's birth in 1983.

During my last visit to Erfurt, without Monika or Horst, I was followed. It was an experience I have never previously been aware of in East Germany, at least certainly not in the conspicuous way it happened this time. My tail was obviously not one of the deadpan members of the State Security service. Such people are instantly recognisable: fit-looking men who smoke too much and look far too nonchalant to be true. This one was an awkwardly self-conscious youth of about twenty, seemingly very preoccupied and mooching along, hands deep in jacket pockets, about twenty yards behind me.

He waited for me to climb the old stone steps up to the cathedral precinct — another evocative moment: there were four nuns, in full habit, just ahead of me — and he was still there when I came out of the Cathedral. (Inside, since the banks were all closed, I changed some West German marks at a rate satisfactory to me and, presumably, to the less-than-rich Church authorities.)

To re-satisfy my curiosity, I retraced some of my steps, taking another look at the old Krämer Bridge, a stone-built structure six hundred years old and still with original houses and shops along each side. My tail mooched a little closer. Then, when we got back to the cathedral square for a second time, he could clearly contain himself no longer.

'Look,' he almost shouted, angrily, obviously intending me to hear him, 'just look at that. It is bad, it is really bad.'

In a country where the majority seem for much of the time to be reasonably satisfied with life, his tone was one of disgust. He was pointing at one of the old merchants' houses which fronted on to the square. It was empty and unused, the timbered upper floor leaning over a ground floor which was a shop. Its windows were impenetrably dirty and the woodwork was rotting and unpainted. The doorway stank.

Its counterpart in Bavaria would have been tarted up (very gaudily, no doubt), but this one stood out as a reproachful symbol of depression and neglect in one of the most prosperous economies in Eastern Europe. 'They'll never fix it,' fumed my tail, 'because they haven't got the money and they've got their priorities all wrong.'

Having divested himself of this very political piece of information, some of the tension went out of him, and he sloped off, a small but unhappy fragment of political opposition. He clearly had nothing to do with any government agency. But in a disciplined society like the GDR, dissent is not easy. The encounter has stayed in my mind.

Certainly it was still with me that evening when I caught a stopping train to Leipzig. The seats were hard and uncomfortable, which didn't bother me too much. But the windows of the carriages were among the dirtiest I have ever seen — dirtier by far than the merchant's shop — and this bothered me quite a bit. Was there nobody, after nearly forty years of the GDR, who was responsible for train windows? Did nobody give a damn?

From Marx to Lenin

The events which were to lead to the formation of the GDR in 1949 started early in the last century in the region I have just described. The first was the defeat inflicted by Napoleon at Jena in October 1806. Another was the defeat inflicted on him at Leipzig seven years and two days later.

Germans, especially East Germans, do not like to dwell on their debt to the French Emperor. But it is a fact that important stirrings of specifically German nationalism, coupled with an implicitly political concern about social conditions, received fresh impetus in the years which followed that defeat. Long before Karl Marx and Friedrich Engels were born, there had been an upsurge in spirit in young Germans, often romantically and unrealistically expressed, and a wish for change.

Freiherr vom und zum Stein, an aristocratic liberal, sought to harness this mood and to forge the required change through offices of state. He did not always succeed, but in 1808 he announced a series of proposals for social reform, envisaging a society that was unashamedly bourgeois with values based on what he construed as freedom and equality. A statue of him now stands on Unter den Linden, in the centre of East Berlin.

Student groups, known as *Burschenschaften*, were formed, starting at the University of Jena and then spreading throughout northern and central Germany. In 1817, these students staged a demonstration of their radicalism, based on Christianity and feeling for the 'fatherland', a concept which has become a source of pride to Germans on both sides of today's divide. Answering a call from Jena, several hundred of them gathered for a rally at Wartburg

Castle. They snaked up the hill, declared effusively for 'the German people' and for national unity, and burned books, including the *Code Napoléon*.

Within a year, this happening had led to the evolution of another movement, also student-led, for the removal of kings and local princes and for the setting-up of a unified German republic. A new nationalism, with all its latent strengths and weaknesses, was in the air.

By the 1830s, there had been a second revolution in France, an uprising in Poland and a surge of nationalism in Italy. All were to find echoes in German minds. Politics became dominated by what West German historians now call 'emotional nationalism', which was a distraction from the needs of those for whom uneven development meant only a deterioration in economic and social conditions. One of a number of cholera outbreaks in the 1830s hit Berlin, and a victim was Georg Hegel, philosophy professor at the still-new university. His scientific and logical teachings on the individual and the state were to influence young Karl Marx when he studied in Berlin (soon after Hegel's death) and have influenced countless others since.

One who did not go along with Hegel and who does not get much of a hearing in East Germany nowadays was the poet and playwright, Georg Büchner. He seemed to be pointing a socialist way forward, nevertheless. In the drive for revolution, he wrote in 1835, relations between rich and poor are the only things that matter. The poet, Heinrich Heine, who was to become a friend of Marx, was moving angrily in the same direction.

By the 1830s, the working population had begun to converge on the towns and cities. Their move was in protest against feudal conditions on the land and in response to the newly forming industrial sector which needed a man-made infrastructure. Here, the workers were exploited — there is no other word — at their place of work and forced to live in hovels or worse, somehow surviving in wretchedly impoverished, overcrowded and disease-prone conditions. Their own spokesmen were few and far between.

Into this sort of climate, into well-to-do bourgeois families, Karl Marx and Friedrich Engels were born and grew up. Separately and together, they were to compile tracts which almost from the start were anathema to the authorities. Neither of them was to spend much of his working life in Germany, and although they have become towering figures in European thought, neither, at first glance, was the sort of material from which revolutionaries are made. Both were to misjudge repeatedly the prospects for real revolution in Europe.

However, both were imbued with compassion for other people in difficult situations — and particularly Engels who was appalled by working-class conditions — even though neither of them spent any time on the shop floor or at the barricades. Both would have fitted well enough into the 'dissident' scene of today's East Europe.

Karl Marx came from a respectable Jewish background. He was in part Jesuit-educated, and a keen student of Greek philosophy. At one time or another during his youth, he went to prison for drunkenness and riotous behaviour, ran up debts (that never stopped), went hunting, fought at least one duel, and wrote bad poetry. He married well, but quarrelled with his parents and, on a grander scale, with the Prussian authorities before being hounded into exile for his political activities.

He lived most of his life in disorganisation, poverty and statelessness. He was intermittently anti-semitic. He suffered from persecution mania and self-pity and had suicidal moments. For a person writing papers which were so brilliant they were to change the course of history, he was very bad at keeping deadlines. He fathered at least one illegitimate child, who was named after Engels.

Engels was more conformist, though he too would have made no headway in today's East Germany. His father was a textile manufacturer who sent young Friedrich to Manchester to turn the British subsidiary into a viable profit-centre. This Engels did, and immediately creamed off a portion of the profits to fund the poorer Marx.

Engels enjoyed the good life, hunting, socialising, and woman-ising, and though he was not as well-educated in the formal sense as Marx — his time in Berlin was in an army barracks — he saw things more clearly, expressed himself more vividly, and applied himself more industriously when the need arose. He seems destined never to achieve the sort of hallowed respect that is accorded to Marx, but it has become clear in recent years that his contributions to political thought were at least as important as those of his partner.

In today's East Germany, the pair are known and spoken of by the leadership as 'the greatest sons of the German people' and streets and squares are named after them in every large town. Marxism, so far as East German students are concerned, is and remains 'the only science' of Communism; Lenin's historical role was to defend the precepts that Marx laid down.

It was in 1848, one hundred and one years before Stalin's generals and some East German politicians announced the formation of the GDR, that the two men set down the challenge of Communism on paper. Neither was yet thirty years old. They did it in London, but their document — the *Communist Manifesto* — was conceived, written and printed in German, compiled by them in exile from thinking based on German experience.

Within a few weeks of the manifesto's appearance, though not in any way influenced by it, Paris exploded. A republic was proclaimed in France and revolution was suddenly sweeping through Europe. Towns and cities throughout the continent were affected, with the poor and the radicals joining assorted others at the barricades against the forces of official law and order.

A succession of bad harvests meant that many of the people who were rebelling were also hungry. Outdated demands for taxes or payments in crops meant that many farmers were angry. Censorship, an unfair legal system and a general lack of workers' rights had many of the intelligentsia up in arms. In some areas, liberals were voted into power, with some worker and peasant support. But the fighting continued — for a year and a half.

East Germany today has its full share of memorials commemorating idealists and others who fell in 1848. In one of the biggest parks in East Berlin, the Friedrichshain, there is a cemetery which contains the remains of 183 of those who died in the struggles of that year.

Erfurt's turn came in November. Walking to the station to catch my train to Leipzig, I came across a plaque high on the wall, at the corner of Anger and Bahnhofstrasse. It listed the names of ten local worthies who had died on 24 November 1848 in the struggle 'for the freedom and unity of Germany'. Speck, the tailor, was one of them, and so was Schwängel, the miller; Engel, the printer, was another, as was Bendhaus, the carpenter. As I took down their names, I wondered what sort of people they were, whether they were people who worked for themselves. It would have been interesting to learn more of their motivation, and whether or not they were socialist, but there was no time.

As I scribbled, an Erfurt couple on their way home paused to see what it was that interested me. I had the feeling that until this moment they hadn't even known the plaque existed, even though it had been there for four decades, put up on the centenary of the incidents described, when the East German wish for unity was strong. It was still nearly a full year before the launching of the people's GDR.

This year of turmoil, 1848, however pointless in the short term, was an amazingly appropriate one in which to offer a Communist manifesto for discussion. (A tract called *The German Ideology* had been produced by Engels a few years before. In places, said the East German historian Franz Mehring at a much later date, it was a puerile work. It had achieved little.)

The manifesto threw an important lifeline to workers and their leaders in many parts of Europe, but in Germany, where Marx had expected the 'final crisis' of capitalism in 1848, it was little read or appreciated. This was partly because some of the suggested strategy had been derived from false or exaggerated premises. The fact had to be faced, both by the German working class in general and by Marx in particular as he returned from Germany to his mean quarters in London, that revolution in the sense of wholesale change was not yet realisable. It was the pressing needs which arose from hunger and an increasing number of mouths to feed rather than any clamour associated with workers' rights that drove the 1848 insurgents to the barricades. Once these barricades were dismantled, the new industrialists — now capitalists — got on with the business of investment and growth. It was not long before Germany's industry was to out-perform the industry of most other European countries.

The East German view today is that 1848 failed because the workers were 'betrayed' by the bourgeoisie. One who tried at about this time not to fail was an intelligent young journeyman printer called Stephan Born. He appreciated what Marx was saying but declined, for fear of exposing himself to ridicule, to call himself a Communist. He facilitated the holding of an inaugural meeting of an organization called the All-German Workers' Brotherhood in Berlin. The workers, especially the skilled workers, responded, and soon there were 170 branches.

A head office was set up in Leipzig and a newspaper was formed. But then, almost as quickly, the Brotherhood, and Born with it, faded. He had decided that he was not, after all, wanting to engage in 'plotting' against the fatherland and that he did not want violence. The Brotherhood became exclusive and started rejecting less skilled workers. In the end, it was to look more like a seed for the Social Democratic Party than for uncompromising Communists.

The Communist League, meeting secretly in London, was the body which commissioned the manifesto, but since the anticipated 'final crisis' had failed to materialise, its tiny membership soon packed up its tents and dispersed. Born had said that Communism was 'centuries' away, and even Engels, long after Marx's death in 1883, was declaring that the manifesto's message was still valid, awaiting implementation. It is, of course, still valid today — an oblique testimony to the durability of capitalism.

Avoiding the issues of a divided Germany, Mikhail Gorbachev, the Soviet Communist Party leader, told the East Germans on his visit in early 1986 that they were doing very well 'in the very homeland of Marx and Engels'. In a break from covering that Gorbachev visit, I went to talk to researchers at the Marx-Engels Institute.

They are engaged, with a parallel team in Moscow, in a mammoth project to collect and collate every single word that Marx and Engels ever wrote. Dozens of 'experts' in East Berlin and Moscow are involved, with teams of up to twenty-five persons at five different East German universities. It has already been under way for more than twenty years and will take until well into the next century to complete. But I came away from this dark and sedate institute wondering whether it was an inner shrine or a forgotten lay-by, and how relevant all this diligent research will be to the needs of the year 2001 and beyond.

In 1853, Engels wrote to Marx that 'the storm was brewing' in Germany but recruitment for the cause was a problem. If Marx had died that year of hepatitis (which he said he nearly did), East Germany's progenitors might have presented a different line-up. The role of Ferdinand Lassalle, for instance, would have to be re-assessed.

Lassalle, seven years younger than Marx, was everything that Marx was not. He was rich, elegantly handsome, popular and witty — and he was in Germany and not in exile when it mattered. He had met Marx in 1848 and was impressed by him. To the older man he appeared to be a hard-working young man of potential usefulness. Within a short period, however, Marx and Engels were petulantly denouncing him, in harshly anti-semitic language, for stupidity, presumptuousness, arrogance, plagiarism and for what Marx read as Lassalle's 'plans to destroy me'. Lassalle, on the other hand, persisted in trusting Marx as far as he was able, while at the same time drawing and organising large crowds every time he spoke on the workers' behalf and selling his writings to many times more readers than Marx could achieve.

To the authorities in Berlin Lassalle's political activities were highly suspect. He did manage to charm Bismarck, then at the head of the Prussian Government, at a number of secret meetings aimed at reconciliation, but he had to move adroitly.

In early 1863, he called for the founding of an independent political party for the working class, and in May of that year, a dozen people met in a room in Leipzig to form the General German Workers' Association (the ADAV), with Lassalle as its first president. The body was non-revolutionary and sought 'by peaceful means' to influence people. It grew and soon had a healthy membership, but Lassalle's role began discomforting the jealous Marx and Engels in the process.

Only when Lassalle died (in 1864, as a result of a duel over a woman) did the pair in England calm down enough to admit that Lassalle, for all his faults, had in fact been a force to be reckoned with on the German scene.

The year after Lassalle's death, Leipzig became the home of Wilhelm Liebknecht. Liebknecht was a cerebral revolutionary who came from a family of scholars, thinkers and civil servants. He was younger than Marx, had taken part in the uprisings of 1848 and had learned his Marxism at Marx's feet, often during picnics on London's Hampstead Heath. Marx thought at first to condemn him, as he had condemned Lassalle, for being 'unreliable and weak-charactered'. But Liebknecht was to become one of the most important and lasting influences inside Germany on the developing workers' movement.

He settled on Leipzig as his base because he was anti-Prussian both in sentiment and in his public utterances. The house in which he lived longest, No. 11 Bräustrasse, opposite a large fruit and vegetable bottling plant, is now a museum. (When I visited it in early 1988, the curator had to break off what was clearly a deep and absorbing conversation with a soulmate to show me round. I stayed for two hours; there were no other visitors in that time. The curator, engagingly munching a large apple as she escorted me, grumbled about the weather and the mess that had been left behind by the 'Karl Liebknecht work brigade' when it redecorated the house.)

Liebknecht had been an early member of Lassalle's new group but was soon disgusted by the 'wretched' state of its constituent local branches (or workers' societies, as they were known) and by the fact that Lassalle had even considered working with Minister-President Bismarck. He also doubted Lassalle's willingness 'to support the revolution' when it came. To sort out the differences between the two of them, Liebknecht had wanted to bring his adversary to Marx for adjudication. But Lassalle was dead, and on his way to martyrdom, a few weeks before the appointed day.

The International Workingmen's Association (now known as the First International) was set up, at British and French instigation, in September 1864. Marx did much of the creative thinking for this organisation and was appointed 'secretary' for Germany. He was characteristically upset that Liebknecht did not give him, in this capacity, enough attention, but later grudgingly came round to conceding that Liebknecht was 'the only reliable contact' in Germany.

Liebknecht had arranged a reprinting of the *Communist Manifesto* in Germany in 1865 and frequently in his speeches referred to Marx's thoughts and theories. He then became Marx's appointed correspondent and plenipotentiary, and soon there was no one inside Germany doing more to promote Marx's interests. This fact alone makes it strange that the Bräustrasse museum is devoted much more to Wilhelm's comparatively headstrong son, Karl, than it is to Wilhelm himself. The probable reason, I later discovered, was that Liebknecht, after starting the radical newspaper *Vorwärts*, tended to lose touch with the grassroots, earning their mistrust and even contempt. Unpardonably, he also became rich and started to live too well for his adopted class.

In 1860, a twenty-year-old itinerant wood-turner called August Bebel had entered the Leipzig scene. He was conservative by nature and though he had joined one of Germany's first workers' educational societies (which flourished where political cells were not allowed) he was reluctant to become political. He even accused the followers of Lassalle of seeking to spread the 'horrors of Communism'. Then, almost as soon as he met Liebknecht, he became a convinced follower of Karl Marx. His unique advantage among the growing band of committed Socialists (of whatever pedigree) was that he was working-class.

On meeting Liebknecht, two days after the latter arrived in Leipzig, Bebel realised he had found a foil and someone who would feed him with ideas. For his part, Liebknecht had found an able organiser who had, through committee memberships, the capability of providing him with public platforms. Both men were anti-Prussian by inclination, in favour of a unified Germany, and both publicly endorsed the teachings of Marx and Engels. It was a remarkable collaboration while it lasted and, separately and together, these two men did more than anyone else on the ground to galvanise the German workers' movement.

Bebel was to move over to the newly formed Social Democrats when they came into being in 1891, but he is still warmly remembered as a revolutionary fighter in today's GDR, probably more warmly than Wilhelm Liebknecht. In one charming East German account, he is depicted in the Imperial Parliament: 'There he sat among princes, barons, and the gentry, among high officials and generals, among bank directors and factory owners and professors, a simple working man — for he had to live on his wood-turning in Leipzig — and represented with all the pride at his command the German working class . . . .' It did not matter to this narrator that he was already sitting as a member for the SPD.

The grumbling confrontation between Liebknecht and Bebel on the one hand and the Lassalleans on the other led to a clash in the summer of 1869. It happened at the Golden Lion on the outskirts of Eisenach, an inn which had been used for the staging of local opera performances, including Mozart, some decades before. More recently it was used by local gymnasts and fire fighters for public displays of their skills. Eisenach was then a tourist resort, and the Golden Lion was chosen for its unobtrusive location. This was good thinking. The clash became something of a drunken brawl, with about a hundred indignant Lassalleans, painfully aware that their efforts to achieve control of the meeting would not succeed, disrupting the proceedings with noisy catcalls and the singing of the workers' anthem of that time, the Marseillaise.

Against them were ranged 263 anti-Lassalleans (shortly to become known as the Eisenachers). Their notional leaders — Bebel, Liebknecht and company — had spent weeks preparing. By the end of the first day they had installed their own chairman, had issued new admission cards to delegates and had booked a room at another inn, the Moor, in Eisenach, where the proceedings could continue. Police moved in to maintain some sort of order, the debate became less strident, and the Bebel-Liebknecht faction carried the day.

The Golden Lion is today no longer an inn, but a museum dedicated to Bebel's move to start 'a greater German working-class party'. It was Bebel — no mention of Liebknecht — who devised the agenda for the meeting and who, once it was over, wrote the programme for the new party, the Social Democratic Workers' Party (the SDAP). The programme, according to the present curator, was 'mainly Marxist'. Marx himself had been invited to attend, but declined, in this curator's version, saying 'the workers' should decide their own fate without him.

The messy triumph for Liebknecht at Eisenach was short-lived. Opposition from the Lassalleans persisted and membership of the new party fell, vitiated on the one hand by the pervasive fever for war against France and on the other hand by effective harassment from the police. Liebknecht was obliged to stomp the country, defining his aims and seeking for unity wherever possible. This included unity against autocratic policies and the machinations of Bismarck in the Reichstag, an institution which at this time he famously labelled 'the fig-leaf of absolutism'.

On the eve of the proclamation of the German Reich in mid-1871, SDAP membership was down to just over 6000 and the circulation of its newspaper down to little over 1000. Arguments intended to incite the populace against the war, propounded by Liebknecht and Bebel, found them both tried in a Dresden court for high treason and sentenced to two-year prison terms. In their absence the Lassalleans' ADAV and Bebel-Liebknecht's SDAP talked about getting closer, even though the continued police harassment, hundreds of court cases and deportation orders made the possibility very remote. On his release Liebknecht was to argue against this fusion — Lassalleans had stoned his Leipzig home for opposing the war — but once they started lobbying him in earnest, he was obliged to change his mind.

It was the 1875 conference at Gotha that finally brought this fusion about. The event caused the immediate displeasure of Marx, though it was a fairly orderly affair. The venue was an inn called the Tivoli, which is situated in a quiet street away from Gotha's pleasant town centre. The Tivoli was run by a Widow Kaltwasser and was a fashionable establishment which included a restaurant on the terrace. Today it is an outwardly plain building, reconstructed inside as another museum, without the terrace. Because Marx was so critical of what happened here, it has also reconstructed itself to become a potted history of the working class movement.

Like so many East European political museums, the Tivoli is a dry affair with lots of reading matter and 'facts', consciousness-raising quotations on every wall. But it is also a more human place than the Golden Lion. Wilhelm Bock, a shoe repairer, opened the conference, so there is a small display of a cobbler's workshop of the time, nails in a tray and well-worn stool and all. Above the bookstall at the door, there are two homely tea-towels, one listing answers given by Jenny Marx (Karl's wife) and the other, by Friedrich Engels, to a dozen or so very human questions. The first tells us that Jenny's 'hero' was Coriolanus and her 'heroine' was

Florence Nightingale. Engels claims to have 'no hero' and as for heroines, says there were 'too many to give a name'.

(The very serious young woman who took me round this time surprised me by having a great deal to say about Lassalle. It was his view, she said, that 'only the working class' was revolutionary. So he excluded himself? 'Yes.' And Karl Marx? 'Certainly.' Then she added that Lassalle was 'very heavily criticised' by Marx, 'but in the 1980s our historic approach has changed, sometimes even considerably. Lassalle's final target was always socialism . . . .')

Since the museum purports to show the history of a whole movement, there is much of Lenin as well as Marx. There is also space for Eduard Bernstein, the thinking gradualist, and later revisionist, who entered the scene about this time. My serious guide made little of the differences that emerged on this occasion between Bebel and Liebknecht and, subsequently, between Marx and Liebknecht for the latter's 'concessions' to the Lassalleans. The 'old man' in London was appalled, as he spelled out in his famous 'critique', that the workers should have endorsed any other road to power than one which was revolutionary. Striving for a socialist society 'by all legal means', as the Gotha conference approved, was not on for Marx. He demanded a 'revolutionary dictatorship of the proletariat', and he and Liebknecht were never completely to trust each other again.

Always, there was the Bismarck factor. He was by now the Imperial Chancellor. It is intriguing to speculate now to what extent the rigours and the repression of the Bismarck era, as well as its empire-building, contributed to the 'character-forming' of today's Germanies. Certainly repression must have sharpened the mind of the conspiratorial and revolutionary elements, and the attention of 'the authorities', even when they were represented by a bevy of heavy-handed policemen breaking up a meeting or making an arbitrary arrest, did much to highlight the importance of what the alleged conspirators were trying to achieve. The fact that Bismarck had the land-owning Junkers on his side, and that the Army and the civil service were largely filled with representatives of this exclusive social group, at the same time gave substance to 'the class struggle'.

Whatever the merits of such arguments, the Socialist Workers'

Party of Germany (the SAPD) was formed at Gotha and it was to gain in votes during the 1870s. The outcome of Gotha may have been compromise, but by the end of the decade there were a dozen Socialist representatives in Bismarck's Reichstag. They gave Bismarck good reason to feel discomforted. The steady proliferation of Socialist publications and the increasing number of speakers who were capable of drawing large crowds at political meetings were added reasons.

Bismarck had tried dialogue with Lassalle, and at one stage had approached Marx himself. Such gestures were made with one hand behind his back and from behind closed doors, for that was his style. Or rather, it was until 1878, the year in which there were two attempts to assassinate Kaiser Wilhelm. The first of these attempts was attributed, in part, to the Leipzig Workers' Educational Society 'directed by Reichstag Deputy Liebknecht'. The second was also attributed to Socialists, and demonstrations to have their members ejected from the Reichstag were organised in the streets of Berlin. By the end of the year, the Anti-Socialist Law was in force, dissolving workers' associations, closing their publications, and giving added authority for arrests, imprisonment and exile.

The only remaining official vehicle for public Socialism was a seat in the Reichstag. The industrial area of Saxony returned six out of nine deputies who kept their seats in elections that year, Bebel and Liebknecht among them. But the law was to remain in force for a dozen years.

Marx died in 1883 but activities in favour of Marxism and other Socialist variations continued underground. Splits in loyalties developed, as Bismarck authorised subsidies to sustain faltering industries and introduced his social welfare reform measures. Such measures, he admitted later, would not have been introduced if there had been no Socialist Party. Increasing numbers of the bourgeoisie came over to his side, abandoning as they did so the more revolutionary Socialist factions. Liebknecht was even driven to conceding — in a Reichstag speech in March 1879 — that his supporters had no plans to overthrow the existing 'social order', Forceful revolution was, he declared, 'after all, an absurdity'.

There is no shortage today of disgruntled, dissident people in Eastern Europe, including odd corners of East Germany, who have suffered at the hands of the security forces of Socialists now in power. They would no doubt recognise the harsh steps then taken by Bismarck's security forces to stamp out Socialism. Homes were destroyed, families broken up, careers and even lives brought to an abrupt end. Many Germans emigrated, never to return.

A law office was established in Leipzig to help the persecuted, but nevertheless more than 1500 Socialists were sent to prison for sentences totalling more than 1000 years, and nearly 900 were thrown out of their own homes. Although today's East Germans like to concentrate on the fact that capitalism was already advancing at that time along the road to its own demise, the pain and anguish suffered by individuals were widespread and real.

The Anti-Socialist Law was finally repealed in 1890. By that year, doubts had grown about Bismarck's ability to keep the growing movement in check. His main patron, Kaiser Wilhelm, had died. After a brief interregnum, the Kaiser's grandson Wilhelm II, making bizarre noises which appeared to be in the workers' favour, had taken over. Bismarck was getting older. More tellingly, the workers' own organisations were gaining numerically and the strikes which they were able to organise were increasingly effective. Elections in 1890 yielded well over 1.4 million votes for Socialist candidates, almost double the figure of three years before. Trade unions took no great interest in Marx or Engels but they now had four times as many members as they had in 1878. Brute force, said Liebknecht on the repealing of the law, had given way to 'the logic of events'.

As Socialism legally re-asserted itself above ground, August Bebel became the central figure. He was uncompromising in his determination not to co-operate with a 'bourgeois' government, preferring to assume that 'the final struggle' was always more or less imminent. He was also a very capable mediator between factions who might be demanding immediate radical solutions and others who might be seeking an unacceptable accommodation with the status quo.

The approved East German view today is that this time was one in which capitalism had left the era of 'free competition' and entered the era of 'reactionary monopolism of the imperialist epoch'. In more readily comprehensible terms, this meant that people were still leaving the land to work in the fast-growing cities, and that autocratic employers were managing to keep the upper hand. They remained hostile to what they saw as political (meaning Socialist) activity and to the steadily growing strength of the trade unions.

Class differences were exacerbated. The average worker, especially if he had a large family, had to live austerely to make ends meet. Poor housing and overcrowding remained huge problems. Women more often than not had to go out to work to keep their families fed. Drunkenness became a major problem for many families. One legacy in today's East Germany is that there are far fewer places to drink than there used to be.

The upstairs rooms in Erfurt's Futterstrasse where, in 1891, Germany's Socialists held an historic meeting to deal with these problems are closed for re-building. A grand centennial re-opening ceremony is due in 1991. The dull grey building in Futterstrasse was boarded up when I went to look, and the modest pillared entrances — even of the inn next door — were firmly shut and padlocked.

Visitors to the building before the recent closure were told that the 1891 gathering was held there to mark the victory of 'the revolutionary German proletariat' over Bismarck and his discredited laws. The programme that this gathering approved, though it brought together a number of apparently irreconcilable points of view, is now seen as the 'best' that could be expected at such a time. It adopted what is today described as a thoroughly Marxist approach, and Engels, still fighting from his London base when he was well past seventy, said that Marx would have been well satisfied. The SPD, which this conference gave birth to, became a major force in West Germany after 1945. In East Germany it was to be consumed by the German Communist Party in 1946.

The Erfurt 'programme' was the work of two men. One was Karl Kautsky, a central European intellectual with romantic inclinations, who was born in Prague and educated in Vienna. He had met Marx shortly before Marx died and proceeded to devote much of his life to interpreting, and popularising, Marx's works. His share of the programme was to highlight the differences between the exploiters and the exploited, and to suggest a timetable for the decline of capitalism, and the ascendancy of Socialism.

The second co-author was Eduard Bernstein, the self-taught son of a Berlin train driver. He was one of the many who had been forced into exile by the 1878 law and befriended Kautsky in Switzerland. He was gradualist by persuasion and in the programme he concentrated on outlining reforms, several of which implied accommodation with those in political power. He advocated proportional representation, for instance, and modifications of income tax, as well as free medical care and the abolition of the standing army.

Later, after he had rubbed shoulders in London with the early Fabians, Bernard Shaw and the Webbs among them, his gradualism was to give way to more unambiguous revisionism. It is ironical to think now that Shaw and the Webbs were themselves later to enthuse about what they perceived as the 'realities' of the Soviet Union under Stalin.

But while the collapse of capitalism in the short-term was taken for granted in the programme, there was, rather astonishingly, once again no mention of revolution nor of how power should be seized. By the time Bebel died in 1913, the SPD was the biggest Socialist party the world had yet seen, a model for Socialists everywhere and, apparently, all things to all men. Except, that is, for the serious would-be revolutionaries. For them, Erfurt was a parting of the ways.

Hindsight and history have made it easier for East Germans and others to select personalities who emerged during this period to influence political development in Germany in what is currently seen as a progressive way. Not unexpectedly, it is those who were to become members of the German Communist Party, when it was formed, who are now seen in the most auspicious light.

Four who did emerge were Karl Liebknecht (son of Wilhelm), Rosa Luxemburg, a Polish-born intellectual, Franz Mehring and Clara Zetkin. None of them was working-class in origin, but all were intellectually committed to fundamental change, aligning themselves sooner or later against the gradualists. All are remembered in today's East Germany with a fair, if not quite wholehearted, measure of respect.

Of the four, Luxemburg was the most formidable. She was a fearsome, single-minded intellectual, a woman of many parts and skills, exciting strong feelings while she was alive but remembered in today's East Germany with some circumspection. If ever Lenin is reappraised enough to grant him a certain fallibility, the strength of Luxemburg's arguments against him (against elitism and in favour, passionately, of mass participation) will also be heard more clearly.

She said at one point her concern was to wake Bebel and his supporters from what she saw as 'his enchanted sleep'. She, in return, was described behind her back as 'a poisonous bitch'. She was also, fascinatingly, one of few personalities in the Communist movement who approached the Renaissance ideal in the diversity of her concerns and interests. No East German full-scale biography of her has yet been attempted.

Liebknecht, who was frequently at her side, was a person of courage and conviction but also of some impetuosity. He is presented as something of a hero-figure in East Germany (as Luxemburg is not), especially for the stand that he made, and encouraged, against the First World War. He would rant in the Reichstag, often in solitary protest, and he would harangue crowds in the street, getting arrested, tried and imprisoned for his pains. He, too, has not yet been probed very deeply, possibly because he was so often thrust into circumstances he would like to have dominated but never did because he was surrounded by more effective thinkers and doers.

Franz Mehring was twenty-five years older than the preceding pair and came to active politics late in life. He was an early example of the radical but broad-minded campaigning journalist that the German scene has thrown up from time to time. He swung over to revolution under Luxemburg's influence, but the pair had an uneasy relationship when it came to journalistic collaboration. His affinity was more with writers like Kurt Tucholsky, who were to emerge in the 1920s, than others, like Marx, who had gone before.

Finally, in this small radical group, there was Clara Zetkin. She outlived them all to defy Hitler (in her seventy-sixth year) from her seat in the Reichstag. She was a village school-teacher's daughter and an active feminist, even from the 1880s, one of few to figure on the German scene at such a time. She also gravitated towards the revolutionary left under Luxemburg's influence and was to make her mark as a journalist and polemicist. If her Communist convictions wavered in the turmoil that followed the First World War, it was conversations with Lenin, not Luxemburgist arguments, that sustained her faith.

Today's memories of all four are selective. There are streets and squares in East Berlin that now bear their names, but there is no statue of any of them and no exclusive museum devoted to their accomplishments. At least three of them have been criticised for not seeing quickly enough through the ploys of the revisionists while at the same time expecting too much from 'spontaneous' mass action.

Lenin, an angry but sick young man in his mid-twenties, was in Berlin a few years after the Erfurt conference on the first of a number of visits he was to make to the city. Every one of these visits is now carefully chronicled — right down to a toy that a host's child put by his bedside in case he was lonely in the night. His main preoccupation was studying and talking, with other Russians as well as German agitators.

He was to cross swords with Luxemburg on a number of occasions. He also formulated a healthy respect for the new SPD. 'We are not in the least afraid to say,' he reported in 1899, 'that we want to imitate the Erfurt programme. There is nothing wrong in imitating what is good, especially today when we hear such frequent opportunist and equivocal criticism of that programme. We consider it our duty to speak openly in its favour.'

In the two decades or so from the Erfurt conference to the outbreak of the First World War, or put another way, from the death of Engels in 1895 to the death of Bebel in 1913, there were to be a number of issues that sharpened the differences that distinguished these three groups. There were those in the SPD who were constitutionally reasonably 'sound' (looked at through Prussian eyes); those who were centrist/revisionist; and those who gathered round the just-named radical quartet.

Representatives of all three groups were capable of getting lost in abstruse polemicising and debate, or in tussles which were remote from the needs and often the understanding of the people in the street. The language of the people, like their needs, was more basic, and their political affiliations were usually easy to recognise — if not coherently expressed. But an attempt by the Kaiser's government to introduce a law against 'subversion', threatening arrest to anyone engaging in Socialist activities, made no impact.

Running through all political arguments was the crucial question about whether or not to work with the middle class. By the turn of the century it had become a substantial, growing and easily recognisable social grouping, often newly rich but invariably people who had profited in all senses from the coming of the Empire. They were a diverse lot, engaged in entrepreneurial development, the service industries, the professions or in the multifarious bureaucracies which had proliferated in Berlin and other cities.

The more their interests grew and the more complex German society became, so the old proposition of Bebel (made in 1884) that the whole edifice of capitalism would soon come 'crashing down like a house of cards' became less and less tenable. Bernstein saw this view as starry-eyed, but then Bernstein was edged to one side, and the central four and their supporters were forced willy-nilly into the role of conspirators. They were lonely conspirators — as Luxemburg, for one, was game enough to admit — and the masses did not heed their calls to revolution or to strike. The confused and unsuccessful attempt at revolution in Russia in 1905 only complicated the German situation. Luxemburg urged the people on, but her critics advised her the Russian situation was not the German situation.

The big strikes came in the end, and were intense and bitter when they did so. The conspirators, or 'intrepid revolutionaries' as East German historians now call them, were angry when war finally broke out in 1914, even though at the outset, war was greeted on all sides with as much enthusiasm as the Kaiser could generate. But as casualties began to mount at the front, so hardships and shortages began to grow at home. As national enthusiasm crumbled, so did the last semblance of SPD unity. The conspirators turned themselves into the Spartacus Group in early 1916. The centrists with whom, try as they might, they could not see eye to eye, met at Gotha a year later to form the Independent Social Democratic Party (the USPD).

As the war progressed, demonstrations and food riots — fuelled by what is now seen as exploitation at the hands of the capitalist manufacturers — were turned into renewed strike actions. Insofar as these actions may now be considered a step towards revolution, the credit is given by the East Germans to the Spartacists. However, the Spartacists at that time were still a comparatively small grouping, and their calls for the strikes to become an uprising which could then somehow become revolution were not heeded by the rank and file strikers. The strikers' prime interest was more food and better living and working conditions.

The USPD today gets short shrift. East German historians say they confused important issues at a fraught time, blurring pacifism with anti-revolutionary tactics. The SPD leadership had come into the hands of the newly appointed Friedrich Ebert, a stolidly unimaginative successor to Bebel. He had tried saddling, editing and a period as an innkeeper before turning to politics and is now routinely castigated for his willingness to allow the SPD to go along with the Kaiser's establishment, and within a very short time, to become that establishment itself. (Ebert's son, also called Friedrich, was a different kettle of fish; he became the first Lord Mayor of East Berlin in 1949.)

In April 1917, Lenin paid his last visit to Germany, stopping once again for a while in Berlin. He still nursed hopes that Liebknecht would lead the country to revolution, even though the main talk among the German Left at this moment was of the newly formed USPD. But Lenin could not communicate. He was in a sealed train and, at the halt in Berlin, his platform at the Potsdamer Station was cordoned off by police to prevent demonstrations. Six months later came the Russian Revolution. And in the wake of that revolution, as one East German historian later wrote, 'Imperial-imperialist Germany was doomed to defeat.'

Second Excursion: Berlin —
The Spaces Between

There are brash tour operators in West Berlin that will take you, at a price, on a whirlwind trip to East Berlin. It is the nearest that many people get to tasting what they call 'Communism'. I tried it once. We were kept waiting while the double-decker bus filled up, but were then taken almost painlessly through the passport formalities at Checkpoint Charlie.

Once through the checkpoint, we were driven through quiet streets in the city centre to the massive Soviet war memorial in Treptow Park, then along the Karl-Marx-Allee, down Unter den Linden, into the old Kaiser's museum complex, past the Brandenburg Gate and out again. It was all done in the gathering twilight of a gloomy, overcast day and to the accompaniment of some totally unsophisticated propaganda from an expatriate apparently born-again American driver. Once back through the checkpoint, he welcomed us back to what he called the 'freedom' of the Kurfürstendamm.

It is the last way I would recommend even a first-time visitor to see the city — unless, of course, one wants to learn something of the quick buck business ethnic which, it has to be faced, has always been part of the city's way of life. Berlin, on both sides, is all about the rip-off.

Above all, this is a city which should be seen on foot, in the company, if all else fails, of a good guide book. But do not go, unless you have to, in the winter. It can be bitterly cold, and the east wind whips mercilessly about the open streets. Revolutionaries who went about these streets in the winter of 1918–19 were often hungry as well as cold; they deserve sympathy on that score at the very least.

I know the city well. But I have always wanted to spend a few hours in its centre, on both sides of the Wall, with someone who was a convinced Communist in the early 1930s. He or she, if they had the energy, would take me to areas which may now have been bombed out of existence, or refurbished out of recognition, and would tell me what happened here or there: about the speech-making, the crowds, the intervention of the 'authorities', latterly wearing brown shirts, and of the confrontation — and the pain — which followed.

Sadly, of course, such people are dying off, or have moved on, or changed their spots. Certainly, if they are in West Berlin or West Germany, they have probably disappeared like insects into the fabled woodwork. If they are in the eastern part, they may have become hard-liners whose real motivation evaporated years ago.

No European metropolis has the peculiar piquancy of Berlin. Since the abrogation of Bismarck's Anti-Socialist Law, it is a city which has probably broken more political promises in the space of a hundred years than the rest of Europe put together. Sightseeing now means being confronted with historical artefacts which may have physically been transported from one part of the city to another. The great statue of Bismarck himself, now faded and barely regarded at a busy traffic intersection called the Grosser Stern in West Berlin, used to stand in feigned splendour in front of the Reichstag. The classical statues, which have been given a good scrub and now grace the Marx–Engels Bridge in East Berlin, were for years kept in store in the West. It is a city of memorials, but a lot of things are not what they seem. It is also a city of silences and empty spaces.

Because the East German travel bureaucracy has not yet come round to the idea of small boarding-houses where I can stay inexpensively and slip away after a quick breakfast, I have tended when in East Berlin to stay at the four-star Palast Hotel: a Western-built construction which stands right at the heart of the Socialist city. Unfrequented by almost all East Berliners (hard currency only), it can be seen as a monument either to the astute business sense of the East German planners or to their lop-sided sense of priorities. However comfortable it may be as an hotel, however imposing it may be architecturally, it is an ideological anachronism.

The diminutive bronze figures of Marx and Engels, which stand a stone's throw away across Karl–Liebknecht-Strasse, must have some wry thoughts.

On a summer's day, you can sit by the small fountain which plays at the hotel's side entrance and watch East Berliners and the tourists who are visiting their capital trundle by. It is hard to believe that this airy, spacious part of the brave, new, Socialist city was once one of its most congested districts. Where today's map shows flower beds and lush swathes of well-groomed grass, crowded with rabbits at dusk, the map of the 1930s has a maze of narrow, busy streets, so close together their names are hard to read.

On further examination, the map also discloses that at the beginning of this century, within just a few hundred yards of this spot, there were three of the Empire's most important buildings, all distinguished in their own right and of a very different character one from the other. For the Kaiser and his administration, they were all important power bases: his own city Palace, the stock exchange, and the city's main cathedral.

By the time Hitler was ready to invade Poland in 1939 and start the Second World War, these buildings still stood, but they were shadows of their former selves. The Führer's own headquarters and those of his closest entourage were a mile or so to the west, not far from the Brandenburg Gate.

The Kaiser's Palace had been the residence of the Hohenzollerns since the fifteenth century and, though it had not been inhabited by them since the abdication of 1918, it was a pile of stonework that was of extraordinary, if inexplicable, sentimental value to Berliners. It was considered by people who knew to be a significant specimen of German architectural history. In the last years of Stalin, the decision was taken to dismantle the structure and all it stood for, and to blow up what remained. By the time of the building's 500th anniversary in 1951, it had been virtually razed to the ground. A teacher friend in East Berlin told me on a recent visit that while this gesture was sacrilege in some Germans' eyes, so far as the old class struggle was concerned, it completed a job which had been begun so clumsily with the attempts at revolution that had followed the abdication.

One of the great balconies from the old Palace has been kept. It is reputed to be the one from which Kaiser Wilhelm II declared, as the First World War got under way, that he knew no parties, only Germans — meaning that anyone worth his salt would not hesitate to come forward and fight for the fatherland. Initially, a lot of people did, but as the war dragged on and realities dawned, they dramatically changed their minds.

More to the point, for today's East Germans, it is said to be from this balcony too that Karl Liebknecht stepped forward to declare that the hour had come for 'a free Socialist Republic of Germany'. This he did after he and a group of supporters had talked their way into the palace and, according to some reports, after Liebknecht himself had spent some time cavorting about the Kaiser's former quarters.

How, I asked my teacher friend, did he make himself heard (the balcony is thirty or forty feet above the ground), and did he know that Philipp Scheidemann, a relative moderate in the SPD, had similarly declared, but without the Socialist overtones, from the Reichstag just a few hours before?

My friend paused for a moment — such thoughts don't often come to the regime's more faithful servants — and said simply: 'Your questions, they are good.'

The old stock exchange was built between 1859 and 1864, a time when capitalism in Germany, almost but not quite an Empire, was flexing its muscles and the working class was beginning to measure the extent to which it was being exploited. From the old prints that can be seen in East Berlin's Märkisches Museum, it was a somewhat Venetian concoction, not unlike the Doges' Palace, and with a columned gallery overlooking the River Spree. It was bombed and shelled during the war and the site was cleared, without a visible tear being shed, to make way for the Palast Hotel.

From the breakfast tables of this always busy hotel, quite deliberately, there are dramatic views across the narrow stretch of water to the great cathedral. I make no claims to understanding the finer points of architecture, but so far as I am concerned this building, which is just a shade higher than St Paul's in London, is impressive and formal — almost 'correct' — in a very German way. Its original design incorporated features designed by the country's favourite early nineteenth-century architect, Friedrich Schinkel, but at the end of that same century, orders were given for it all to be pulled down and completely rebuilt.

Now, the rigid geometry of its lines and the uncompromising nature of the stone of which it is made contribute to this Germanness. There is also the fact that the visitor, if he does not cross Karl-Liebknecht-Strasse, which runs alongside, or does not retreat across the remaining fragment of the old Lustgarten park next door, is invariably right up against the building. It is impressive and oppressive at the same time, a view which many in positions of authority in East Germany might also hold to be true of God himself.

For reasons I have yet to fathom, this cathedral was something the authorities decided to keep. It was severely damaged during the Second World War — more severely, I am told, than the Palace opposite — but thoughts which were entertained of demolition were rejected. There have been further modifications to the outside, with some saintly bits of decoration and some of the more grandiloquent crosses removed, but the inside is very gradually being restored. Occasional services are held in the crypt, but the great yawning inside walls of the church have been covered with scaffolding and there has been the continuous noise and dust of reconstruction since 1973. When I last looked in, in 1987, it was all rather a mess, but a mess which would have made a great stage backcloth of some sort. It is also a mess being largely financed, as so much East German church work is, by West German church authorities.

This book could not and would not have been written were it not for the fact that today's city of Berlin is a place — or rather, an environment — which I never tire of walking round, visiting and revisiting odd corners where historical events, some of them notorious, took place. Solicitous East German officials, usually, have been delighted by my interest in their capital and I have spent hours discussing it with anxious hosts in sanitised beer houses. On occasion, they have deputed a friendly guide of their choice to take me round, even an expensive car to whisk me here or there. But this has not worked.

Just as there are gaps between the houses and the public

buildings, which can be startling in their abruptness, so there are gaps, often quite unintentional, in the conversation. Partly this is the result of a selective Marxist education, partly of unsubtle selectivity in thinking. Sometimes, as when the discussion comes round to precisely why the royal palace was demolished, it is something of each. Either way, it can lead to moments of irritation and others of strange mystification.

The Alexanderplatz, or 'Alex' as it is affectionately known, is situated a few minutes' walk to the east of the Marx-Engels complex and was once one of Prussia's several parade grounds in the city. It takes its name from Tsar Alexander I of Russia (hardly a consistently good friend of the Germans) and served for a time as a cattle-market before it became a traditional haunt and meeting place of working-class Berliners.

Today it is a windswept open space punctuated with department stores, public buildings and, once again, a huge international hotel. A colossal statue of the city's mother figure, Berolina, was bombed to smithereens in 1944, and from this moment the spirit of the GDR took over. A complicated clock, which gives the time for any named place in the world, has taken the mother figure's place.

The poverty and the overcrowding which characterised this part of the city in the last century, and which towards the end of it so angered Rosa Luxemburg, have naturally gone. So has the headquarters building of the city police force, an important focal point for discontent and public agitation in the months after the First World War. Today, there are a few market stalls, tucked away behind the Alexanderplatz railway station, but there is no bustle. There is otherwise almost nothing to suggest that this was once one of the most socially significant and vibrant parts of the old city.

Not far from the Alex, to the north, is the old Scheunenviertel, where mournful four or five-storey blocks of flats, their dull grey plasterwork cracked or gently falling away, dominate the urban landscape. It still seems an overcrowded part of the city, mean in the way that old parts of Glasgow are also mean, with alleyways running through to dank, sunless courtyards and more flats, which, however well furnished with inherited bits and pieces, must also be gloomy on even the brightest of days.

Not far from here Horst Wessel, the no-good youth whom Goebbels and the Nazis turned into a hero, had his haunts, and not far from here he was buried. I have looked for the grave — out of curiosity — and have of course found no sign, just as in today's East Germany there seems to be no one one can turn to for further information on such a matter.

More to the point, it was in this immediate vicinity that the Communist resistance was at its most effective. The Party's underground activities thrived in these back streets and warrens, and though the Nazis could storm and take over the nearby Communist Party offices, as they did early in 1933, they could never manage to halt completely the activities or break the spirit, or the determination, of the individual fighters.

Other roots of East German Socialism can be found in the Friedrichstrasse and Oranienburgerstrasse area, which lies north of the Marx-Engels complex, between the Scheunenviertel and the 1961 Wall. This was the stamping ground of Bertolt Brecht and was where many of Berlin's Jews lived before they went into enforced exile, or were taken off to concentration camps and probable death.

Many of these Jews were also Communists and Hitler did not hesitate to blur and confuse the distinction between the two. Both were the common enemy. Today's East Berliners have only a handful of Jews to look after, a few hundred compared with a total of 160,000 in the city when Hitler came to power.

Oranienburgerstrasse houses what remains of the great main synagogue of Berlin, sacked on the Reichskristallnacht of 1938, the same night that so many Jewish shops, businesses and other institutions were sacked. The East German leadership, nearly fifty years after these grisly events, has decided to refurbish the synagogue, and invited Western Jews to come to ceremonies marking their new-found enthusiasm. Many who came, having suffered so much, were grateful. Others were politely guarded in their views; others stayed away.

Friedrichstrasse, close by, retains more than almost any other street in the city centre the sort of spirit — racy and seedy at the same time — which Weimar-era Berlin must have exuded. During the day, it is always full of people. Possibly because it is at the very centre of the East German entertainment industry, it is permeated by a sense of expectation. In the inter-war period, parents and grandparents of the people who now fill its pavements saw some of the finest pieces of theatre that Europe could then offer. Between the famous crossing point at the railway station — which in its very gauntness cannot fail to evoke thoughts of the Cold War — down to the bend in the road where Chausseestrasse begins, there is something in the air which is essential Berlinisch.

The area was important from the beginning of this century for the range it offered in a good night out. There were beer houses galore and prostitutes in and around the small hotels where no questions were asked. There were circuses, music halls and theatres. There were restaurants for the well-to-do and patches where barrel-organ players and beggars ruled. I met an old man in a brand new council house at Marzahn, an estate still going up at the eastern extremity of the city, and he reminisced to me at great length about this street as it then was. His memory for detail, about which building stood where, was now hazy, but when it came to nostalgic rhapsodising, there was no stopping him. He was a Berliner to his finger tips, remembering with appropriate impreci-sion the all-consuming love of his life.

Although some of the most famous playhouses in theatre history have now been pulled down, there are others. The Friedrichstadtpalast is now the city's main centre for shows of all sorts. Here, astonishingly in this often straitlaced country, the dancing girls wear only sequins, and sometimes no sequins at all. It was re-opened by the Party leader, Erich Honecker, in 1984, when he promised that the Friedrichstrasse had a great glittering future.

Nearby is the Theater am Schiffbauerdamm, where Brecht was director and where his plays, of arguable relevance now that the changes he sought have been achieved, are still performed. There is also to be a new Winter Garden, where afternoon tea dancing and entertainment could be revived. The shady hotels and eating houses still exist, as well as, I am told, for those who know where to look, male and female prostitutes.

Outside this central area of East Berlin, and apart from the pre-nineteenth-century contributions along and adjacent to Unter den Linden, there is one intriguing category of building. It relates directly to the Hitler period: buildings that either survived his war or were conspicuously lost as a direct result of it.

The centrepieces are large creations which were erected or came into use during the Nazi era and which have now been taken over and made use of by the Socialist Unity Party, the SED, administration which runs the city and East Germany. First, there is the Party headquarters, situated on the Werderscher Markt, two minutes' walk away from the main cathedral to the south. It is housed in the building commissioned by Hitler to house the Reichsbank, a plain expressionless four-storey edifice in light grey, suitably inscrutable for a building that has seen such a dramatic change of use.

Second, there is the building that was erected at the western end of Leipzigstrasse in the mid-1930s to contain the air force headquarters of the Third Reich under Marshal Goering. Here were prepared the great plans to bomb London and Britain into surrender in the early stages of the Second World War. The building now stands in the shadow of the 1961 Wall and contains the offices of several GDR Government departments. It is known by the near-anonymous title of the House of Ministries.

Third, there is the building, completed as Hitler became Chancellor, which was used in his time as a central clearing house for medical insurance. It is now the SED's Party High School, situated on the Rungestrasse, not far from the Märkisches Museum.

The main Hitler buildings which did not survive were either wrecked beyond use by British and US bombers from the air, or smashed by Soviet shells as Red Army tanks closed in on the innermost core of the city in the last weeks and days of the Second World War. This core was strategically named the 'citadel' by the Wehrmacht, and the buildings in it — including Hitler's chancellery, his bunker, and some very fine properties he had taken over in what was then called Wilhelmstrasse (now Otto-Grotewohl-Strasse) — finished, at best, as unrecognisable skeletons of their former selves.

Many have been cleared away on the backs of lorries or ploughed into the ground. The sites of several have been built on already. The great concrete lumps of Hitler's bunker are being cleared to create a landscaped park. But the substance, as well as the memory, lingers on. At Thälmannplatz underground railway station, as at the Soviet war memorial which stands in the western sector beyond the Brandenburg Gate, the vivid reddish-brown granite is stone salvaged from Hitler's chancellery.

Separating Legend from Fact

Every so often in East Germany, I have met some extraordinarily tough representatives of the older generation, men and women with vice-like handshakes who seem to have fought with every fibre in their bodies against the evils of Hitler. Some have told me how their parents or grandparents participated in the German 'revolution' of 1918–1919, insisting that that time, rather than 1945 or 1949, was the golden hour. It was, they say, when the Great War ended that the old order was overthrown and the Republic proclaimed. The fact that in the new republic it was the Social Democrats who gained the upper hand over out-and-out, but more confused, Socialists is not dwelt upon. What mattered was that the workers' representatives had taken power.

For these dedicated survivors, as for almost everybody else in today's East Germany, the difficulty now is separating legend from fact. Just as students in Britain now know that making the British Empire was not one long adventure but was often shameless and arrogant imperialism of the worst sort, so, more and more, German students are learning of their famous revolution that, in the words of one who took part, 'it is doubtful whether it deserves the name of revolution at all.'

German political history between the two wars has become a grey area with carefully selected highlights. East German commentators exercise understandable care with these highlights, but one result is that there are many highly educated East German citizens — including opinion-formers in the ruling party and in the administration — who have enormous gaps in their knowledge. The interested Western reader may not take much exception, though he or she may argue with, the 'highlights' chosen in the new few pages, but they will be greeted, I know, with a scepticism tinged with incredulity by many East German friends.

At the end of the First World War, many rank and file Germans, like others who went through that war, were hungry, sick, disenchanted and very tired. Even so, for the small number of Communists and others on the political Left, revolution was the stuff of conversation, of everyday life. Reverberations from Russia, where the cerebral Lenin was now in control, were vivid in many ears, but Russia's revolutionaries desperately needed evidence of European support. The effort required from the Germans, the planning that was essential, and the always lurking violence in the city streets, sapped the strength of even the strongest.

Lenin's name remains as formally respected, if not hallowed, in modern East Germany as it is in Gorbachev's Soviet Union. He was in Berlin and other cities a number of times before 1917 and also stayed at mountain resorts that were fashionable with the Austro-Hungarian upper classes. Every one of his movements has been thoroughly documented, and museums created in his honour. Some East Germans concede that he was a controversial as well as an accomplished revolutionary, but few will acknowledge — as one German who knew him well did later acknowledge — that until 1917 he was largely unknown in Germany and Europe and that he was 'certainly without important influence' for most of the German population.

When Lenin's famous sealed train was held up for some hours in Berlin on its way from his Swiss exile to the Finland Station in April 1917, there was interest and curiosity, but there was not great clamour for him to be seen or heard. The train was sealed as a result of an agreement between Lenin's group, the Swiss and the German authorities. Part of the agreement was that there would be no passport or customs control en route, and also that Lenin and company would agitate, once they reached Russia, for the release of a number of Austro-German prisoners-of-war.

News of the revolution in October 1917 came sketchily to Germany. Although some Germans had taken part, the Kaiser's administration had ruled against publishing any explanation or praise of the revolution's progress. But he was unable to stop

Russian newspapers, and some eye-witness accounts, from getting through. Rosa Luxemburg, like Karl Liebknecht, was in prison when it happened, for treasonable activities. She read Russian and was able to lay her hands on reliable evidence.

After months of reflection, she was able to declare that the revolution was 'the mightiest event of the World War' and that the Bolsheviks had done what they had to do. But it was also an event which brought her deep unhappiness and plunged her, once again, into conflict with Lenin. She had already expressed disapproval of the notion of a party elite which Lenin called the 'vanguard'. Now she announced that freedom 'only for the supporters of the Government' or members of one party was 'no freedom at all'. Her analysis was not published in East Germany until 1975. It amounts, after all, to an indictment, a sacrilegious assault on the most sacred of shrines.

In the arguments which followed the signing of the Russian-German peace treaty of Brest-Litovsk, German workers said they had been betrayed because of the opportunities the treaty gave the German ruling class to stabilise and re-consolidate its position in the economy and society. Leon Trotsky, one of the treaty's chief negotiators, wanted to deploy Soviet troops on 'a revolutionary offensive' into Germany at the earliest opportunity, but Luxembourg maintained not only that had the revolution gone wrong in some ways in Russia, but also that Germany was not ready for revolution. With the latter point, Lenin did not disagree.

Lenin, though, looked to Liebknecht rather than Luxemburg to lead a German revolution. 'We know he will be victorious,' he wrote, 'that his revolution in Germany will liberate us from all international difficulties . . . .' Certainly Liebknecht had been an enthusiastic supporter of Russian revolutionary moves in 1905 and he had been vociferous in opposition to the Kaiser, his Government and his war. He had also been silent, or less than critical, towards Lenin and his revolution. Yet he lacked a final dimension — the greater 'vision' of Luxemburg. He was better at haranguing his supporters rather than actually leading them to uncertain barricades. Even so, it makes some sense that he figures more prominently as martyr in today's East German history books than the contentious Luxemburg.

Germans had become polarised early in 1917. On the one hand, they were urged on by newly formed groups of Independent Socialists (the USPD), including the Revolutionary Shop Stewards, who were especially active in the industrial centres. On the other hand, they were held back by the forces, still, of the Kaiser's establishment and of law and order, men who were harsh in the extreme, who cut the bread ration by half and punished demonstrators with conscription.

Though some of the conscripts raised red flags on the trains taking them to the front, and though many still flocked, almost instinctively, to political meetings, not many knew very much about the Spartacists, as the Communists still called themselves. The authorities, however, felt they had the measure of the Spartacists. They saw them as disruptive and subversive elements.

The war in its final phase was a ragged affair, protracted by an obdurate and unreasonable Kaiser, aided and abetted by even more obdurate officers. One was Field-Marshal General Paul von Hindenburg, a war-horse, already past seventy years of age, an old Prussian junker who remained a pillar of the establishment — and the monarchy — until his death many years later. He now wrote impatiently to General Wilhelm von Gröner, based in Berlin, demanding that the restive workers in the city should be 'enlightened'. Von Gröner needed little prompting. On receiving this letter, he publicly declared that Germany's worst enemies were not at the front but 'in the midst of us'. They were leading strikes.

The workers were incensed and, for a while, Berlin was perilously close to civil war. Half a million of them, it has been estimated, poured onto the city streets, overturning buses and trams and paralysing transport. Since many were in the armaments industry, arms were 'found' to add to those appropriated, with minimal ceremony, from troops on leave. Shock militia units were formed — by both sides. Confronting the workers were semi-official armed squads, to be known as the Freikorps, men who remained loyal to the pre-war order of things, and were later to form the kernel of the relentlessly anti-Communist Nazi stormtroopers.

Polarisation did not make the political situation any less confusing. When members of the SPD, who had not so long ago voted for arguments of a Marxist flavour, opted to join the Imperial Government of Prince Max von Baden, shortly before the final armistice, Spartacists, Shop Stewards and the rest could be forgiven for thinking it was to be revolution or nothing — now or never.

In the headlong series of events over the next year or two, it was both and neither. The Russian cry — which still echoes today — that since the working class had taken power in Russia, the workers of the whole world had to become Russian patriots, had a certain appeal. But Russia was Russia and Germany was Germany, and in Germany, as Lenin noted, organised state capitalism, directed by a confident upper class, was depressingly well-equipped — and entrenched. Though the Kaiser was eventually forced to abdicate, the Generals and others of their sort remained. When the final mutinous uprising of Kiel sailors took place — they refused to carry out a last order to attack from their imperialist masters — the violence, bloodshed and death which ensued was to pit German against German in often remorseless fury.

In what might be described as a gentlemen's agreement, Chancellor Prince von Baden handed power to the dour Friedrich Ebert. He was a provincial tailor's son who had taken over the SPD at the death of Bebel in 1913, and largely as a result of his capability as an organiser, he had been prominent in the SPD hierarchy since the beginning of the century. Officers and men who had been loyal to the Kaiser immediately switched loyalty to his administration, and, in the words of one astringent observer (the artist, George Grosz), the frock-coated Ebert became less and less representative of the people and more and more like a managing director.

While Ebert fought to keep control, the Russian Embassy, a former royal palace on Unter den Linden, was a hive of activity. Couriers carrying mysterious boxes and bags were seen passing through its doors at all hours of day and night. 'There are reports,' wrote one irate Englishwoman who was in Berlin at that time, 'that it is full of ammunition and weapons, and we suspect that it is a hotbed of Bolshevism and anarchy .... Liebknecht is seen to be constantly going in and out of it, and publicly proclaims his anarchistic (sic) views.'

Thirty years later, there were to be suspicious eyes on the

Russians once again. Undoubtedly they were busy again, and it was Western generals and politicians, rather than shocked wives, who were shaking their fists. The old palace known to Liebknecht was, however, badly damaged and soon had to be bulldozed out of existence. The vast and grandiloquent Soviet Embassy which now stands on the site was one of the first 'new' buildings in Soviet-occupied East Berlin.

Reaction in Russia to the confused events in Germany of 1918–19 was in some quarters in marked contrast to German reaction to Russian events the year before. 'Tens of thousands of workers burst into wild cheering. Never have I seen anything like it. Until late in the evening, workers and Red Army soldiers were filing past. The world revolution had come, the masses had heard its iron tramp, and our isolation was over . . . .'

These were the words of Karl Radek, a colourful and talented figure who for some years had been flitting (on Russia's behalf) like a ghost through Germany. He was a wiry, witty man, a pipe-smoker who favoured bowler hats and was described by a friend as 'one of the brains of the revolution'. Trotsky, whom he accompanied at the Brest-Litovsk peace talks, wrote afterwards that Radek was endowed with 'very lively intelligence and political loyalty' as well as the 'right sort' of energy and passion for the Soviet cause. At this juncture, he probably knew more about Germany than any other trusted Russian of the time. He was the first 'man from Moscow' to have some say in shaping events in Berlin.

Radek was born in the city of Lvov, now part of the Soviet Union though still regarded by many Poles as Polish. Perhaps because they were fellow Poles, he and Luxemburg did not get on together. He was not always predictable, and his wit could sometimes turn to garrulity, his satire to sarcasm. When war broke out, he was expelled from Germany for disseminating anti-militarist propaganda; but at the Brest-Litovsk negotiations, almost the first thing he did on arrival was to open his luggage and distribute, there and then, revolutionary pamphlets to waiting German soldiers.

He had the trust of Lenin, and once the war was over was an automatic choice to represent Soviet interests in Berlin. Radek was the only one of the deputed handful to get through, disguising himself as a returning prisoner-of-war. On arrival, he straightaway launched himself into criticisms of Luxemburg, Liebknecht and others for their lack of 'revolutionary thoroughness'.

Liebknecht, however, was more concerned to denounce Ebert as a 'menace' to the revolution and Ebert was forced to confide in von Gröner his fears of 'the Liebknecht mob'. He then called on the ruthless and, it transpired, bloodthirsty Gustav Noske, an SPD man who had become the new republic's Defence Minister, to restore order. Here and elsewhere in his administration, Ebert was reassured to find that the civil service which had obeyed the Kaiser was still largely intact — and loyal. In the face of such an administration, with Noske's men to the fore, revolutionaries could make little real headway.

On 24 December 1918 Ebert's men stormed the Marstall, an annexe of the Royal Palace, and re-possessed it from armed soldiers, sailors and others who had been holding it for the revolution. In spite of this setback, a stormy meeting was held seven days later, attended by a hundred or so Spartacists, USPD members and Revolutionary Shop Stewards, and the German Communist Party (the KPD) was formed. Such a party was a new phenomenon in Europe, but within only two weeks, it was plunged into catastrophic disarray. Luxemburg and Liebknecht were seized by a Freikorps unit from a flat where they were hiding, dragged off for interrogation and brutally murdered. Ebert himself was shocked by their deaths, but the following month the men who had led that operation had also seen to the arrest and imprisonment of Radek.

From approximately this point, the ups and downs of Germany's Communist Party were a constant preoccupation in Moscow. There was to be sporadic and vigorous resistance from the Germans to interference from the Kremlin, often over the view that membership of the Communist International, established under the Kremlin's auspices, meant conforming to the wishes of the Kremlin. There was to be divergence from the Moscow line, but always — and especially after Stalin's takeover — there was to be a Soviet Russian brake or a Soviet Russian accelerator to control progress. The mechanics today are much more complicated and the Soviet driver is a more sophisticated animal. But there is also a clever East German co-driver and it would not be true to say the situation looks the same today. Soviet control is nothing like all-embracing.

From its earliest beginnings, the KPD was a party torn between extremes. There were factions who were vociferously insisting on immediate revolution, but there were also those against precipitate action. Faithful to Luxemburg's precepts, these groups were against the summary overthrow of Ebert and wanted to prepare 'the masses' by assiduously cultivating them in the factories and at street meetings. There was no chance of any reconciliation with the SPD. Formally speaking, the aim of the latter, despite the frock-coated distractions of the new ruling group, was 'the spiritual, political and economic emancipation of the toiling masses', to be achieved by parliamentary means. The SPD and the other bourgeois parties, on the evidence of votes cast during the 1920s, remained far stronger than the Communists and their supporters. With the traumatic removal of Liebknecht and Luxemburg, one era ended and a new one, characterised by guerrilla tactics from Left and Right, began. The 'political murder' became a political weapon.

Some commentators speak of the 'lost German revolution' as continuing almost non-stop for several years after the end of the First World War. Today's East Germans see things differently. In early 1988, some ponderous 'theses' were published to mark its seventieth anniversary and in November of that year a ceremony was held in East Berlin. But the ceremony was low-key and for today's rationalisers, the creation of the Communist Party was 'the main achievement'.

Radek was imprisoned — for using a false name — rather than murdered because he was seen by the authorities as a contact between Germany and the Bolshevists in Moscow. But while in prison he also did much to foster the fledgling Party (which at one stage he aspired to lead). In reporting back to Moscow — as so many Soviet emissaries must have done since — he offered an idio-syncratic view of the Germans: 'That's the way they all are, these Germans, they think, talk and talk, and the mills never stop turning until others run right over them.'

Day in, day out, Radek did his utmost to encourage a German revolution, arguing that the Communists and the trade unionists should make common cause. As an executive of the Communist International, he enthused on behalf of the Germans and led Trotsky and Grigori Zinoviev, in the Soviet party hierarchy, to do likewise. By 1923, when the disillusion and the bitterness brought on by the war had spread like an infection to become for many a disenchanted and bitter peace, the KPD leadership was summoned to Moscow and placed under pressure to prepare, in October that year, for what the Soviet leadership forecast would be Germany's '1917'.

When the Communists signally failed to take over, Radek, for all his gifts, was made the prime scapegoat. He was to die later in one of Stalin's camps. Trotsky — whom Radek had seen as Lenin's successor — and Zinoviev also fell dramatically out of favour. The creeping rehabilitation in Moscow of Trotsky and others (in late 1988 and early 1989) has thrown modern East German thinkers into sudden spasms of introspection.

KPD tribulations in the party's first years were not helped by Lenin's decline through ill-health. Infighting arose in part because it was an untried and inexperienced organisation. Of course there was a willingness to enter the lists for a loosely identified cause, but there was disagreement after Luxemburg and Liebknecht over who should take the lead. A succession of men and women nailed their colours to the leadership mast, but not all are remembered with equal fervour today. The one remembered most vigorously, Ernst Thälmann, a docker from Hamburg, is honoured more as a great agitator — and later victim of the Nazi concentration camps — than as a thinker. Others are remembered, but none is honoured in quite the same way. It is a fact for which the selective whims of Stalin as well as the selective memories of GDR historians must be taken into account.

Paul Levi was the first to come forward. He was a banker's son and something of an aesthete. He was a moderate by inclination but had taken over the vacant leadership at Luxemburg's death. Like Liebknecht, he was a lawyer, but he was also rich and widely read, and a brilliant speaker, writer and debater.

In due course, however, he was criticised for the party's

'passivity' when confronted with the extraordinary opportunities presented by the brief-lived putsch of Wolfgang Kapp. The latter was an over-zealous and crudely nationalist civil servant who seized power in Berlin in early 1921 and clung to it for a few days largely because he had armed support. Levi came out against proposals for mass strikes during 1921 and, more important, was anti-Moscow and anti-Zinoviev (the Comintern chairman) in particular. Though he often listened to Radek, he went so far as to attack Bolshevism as being 'Asiatic' and, to bolster criticisms of the efficacy of 1917, published his own edition of Luxemburg's thoughts on the revolution. After a year or so, opposition to his leadership was such that he and a small band of right-wing supporters were forced to join the USPD and, some months later, the SPD. He committed suicide in 1929, a puzzling personality to the end, who was unable to control a potentially powerful political force. He was mourned at his death by socialists of every hue as one who had been a fighter against German militarism.

Heinrich Brandler, who succeeded him, was from the Sudetenland and never became a German citizen. His political beginnings were in the industrial town of Chemnitz, where he was a builder. He was one of the first ranking German Communists to articulate a personal pride in being from 'the working class', a social grouping whose capabilities, in his view, the Russians never properly understood. One who had tried to understand was Radek; another, after the death of Lenin and after some initial hesitation, was Stalin.

In 1923, when many in Moscow and in Berlin were agitating for the definitive move by the KPD, Brandler hesitated. Summoned to Moscow that summer, according to one (not impartial) account, 'he got the shock of his life'. Soviet enthusiasm for the German cause had been orchestrated so that the city was plastered with slogans, banners and streamers to the effect that 'the German revolution was approaching'. Pictures of Clara Zetkin, Rosa Luxemburg and Karl Liebknecht were in many shop windows and shopfloor meetings were being called, to discuss ways of 'helping the German revolution'.

When, after much argument, Brandler took his leave, Trotsky kissed him on both cheeks. 'Knowing both men well,' wrote Ruth

Fischer later, 'I could see that Trotsky was really moved; he really felt that he was launching the leader of the German revolution on the eve of great events.' More tendentiously, the same witness adds that she walked past this touching scene 'in the bitterest of moods' and was 'fully convinced that we were running towards disaster'.

When Germany's '1917' did not happen in 1923, it was Brandler's turn to join the ranks of the scapegoats, even though he had never fully gone along with Soviet wishes and prognostications. He had tried to advocate a closer relationship between the Party and the trade unions. The Party, no longer amenable to reason, turned against him.

Sooner or later, no doubt, glasnost or its German equivalent will allow for Brandler the reappraisal he deserves. Certainly, under his leadership, the party made impressive organisational progress. It gave legal aid to political prisoners and succour and support to their families, organised educational classes for those who wanted them, and set up, in spite of ideological differences, a number of support groups for the 'new Russia'. There was a highly developed press service, with thirty-four daily newspapers, a string of polemical pamphlets on Soviet themes, translations from the Russian, and Russian and Soviet films and concerts. There was an organisation formed for Young Communists and another for Communist Women. In some eighty German town councils at this time, the Communists had an absolute majority. Their greatest strength was apparent in Berlin, Hamburg and the Rhineland.

But, as indicated, 1923 was the pivotal year. Staggering inflation meant that as many as 60,000 million marks were needed to make one dollar. There were regular and bloody left-right clashes in the streets, and hungry people were unhindered as they looted shops. Hitler was stirring in the political undergrowth, and there was some talk of the Kaiser being reinstated. When French troops moved into the Ruhr, however, Stalin, in a letter to Zinoviev and Nikolai Bukharin (who had also served a spell in Berlin), wrote: 'If today the (German) Communists seize power . . . they will fall with a crash. The Germans, in my opinion, must be curbed.'

The 1923 uprising failed in spite of the presence of Soviet experts on German soil. Plots to assassinate General Hans von Seeckt, head of the armed forces, and Hugo Stinnes, a leading industrialist, failed. Von Seeckt, on the orders of Chancellor Gustav Stresemann, bounced back to order the immediate banning of the KPD. For working-class Germans it was a time when bitterness could only grow.

The banning of the KPD was a watershed in German political development. The Soviet writer Ilya Ehrenburg, who witnessed these events, wrote that the city was like one huge waiting-room, where nobody knew what the day would bring. He waited 'like everybody else' for the great upheaval which did not come. Instead, the party was obliterated overnight and for six months, as sinister right-wing forces consolidated their various holds on German society, all human traces of it were hounded from pillar to post. KPD members, like dissidents in some East European countries today, operated furtively, risking arrest and persecution. Only their resolution was undiminished: they may have been beating different paths, but they were heading still in the same direction.

The year 1924 saw Brandler summoned again to Moscow. This time he was ordered to keep out of German politics, and the field was wide open for a variety of personalities to vie for the leadership. Arkady Maslow (a Russian) and Ruth Fischer (an Austrian) fought together, sometimes viciously, from the Left and seemed to make headway. From an ill-defined central position, Ernst Thälmann did likewise. So did Wilhelm Pieck and Walter Ulbricht, two men who were eventually to have decisive roles in the country's history. All of these, in different ways, were to be manipulated by Stalin, but all had central roles in the KPD's struggles with the Nazis and their early bids for total control.

It is difficult to measure how great a blow to Germany was Lenin's death in early 1924. He died knowing the KPD had been outlawed and that membership had fallen dramatically. He had never underestimated the potential of the 'counter-revolution' in Germany. As he left the stage, he saw that German workers were turning to the more moderate SPD, and that a new breed, flaunting itself under a National Socialist flag, was moving to the front.

Against Lenin's wishes (as later became clear) Stalin moved up to fill the gap. To begin with, he knew little about German developments and played almost no part in early debates on the 'German question'. Through intermittent intelligence brought to him by Zinoviev and Radek, still occupying positions of some trust, as well as strategically deployed 'agents', he was able to build up his knowledge and to act accordingly.

Stalin's profile became clear for the first time internationally at the World Congress of Communists which was held in Moscow in mid-1924. Ruth Fischer, ambitious and also subjective in her judgments, saw him as 'a new type of Russian leader who despised rhetoric and was a down-to-earth organiser'. Zinoviev, by contrast, she saw as still surrounded by people who were 'old, fussy and outmoded'.

Fischer had her own reasons to curry favour with Stalin. With Maslow, she capitalised on what they both saw as Brandler's 'sell-out' to the SPD, playing off faction against faction until they reached a central position with some control. For two years, she was a member of the Comintern executive, while at the same time a deputy to the German Reichstag, and became acquainted with almost all the early Soviet leaders. As she watched totalitarianism and the philosophy of socialism in one country transform Soviet politics, and the Comintern as well, she became increasingly critical but also inextricably involved herself. Finally, however, she was forced to complain that the 'continued submission of German communism to the Soviet politburo would be disastrous and would end in catastrophe'.

Her turn to fall out of favour came as irrationality took over. She maintained contacts with selected Moscow friends throughout her life, and possibly because she had these friends, Stalin was forced to clip her wings and those of Maslow with her. In the trials of 1936 both were condemned in their absence, charged with having sent an agent to the Soviet Union to murder Stalin. Zinoviev, Radek and countless other German supporters were similarly condemned, to be executed or die in circumstances which only came to light — almost unreported in the East German press — more than fifty years later.

Thälmann inherited the Fischer–Maslow mantle. Born in Hamburg in 1886, and only minimally educated in the formal sense, he started his political life with the Social Democratic Party when he was a young seaman. In the confusion after the war, he went over to the Independent Social Democrats, before moving on to join the Communist Party in 1920. From then, he grew into a political figure of some substance, organising strikes, leading pitched battles against the Right, and delivering himself of a stream of hugely forceful though barely eloquent political speeches.

He was a popular leader, under-educated, self-taught and without any social niceties. But he was full of energy and ideas. Though he spoke vigorously against Soviet erosion of German KPD autonomy, he was spotted early by Stalin and shamelessly cultivated by him. He was given and apparently enjoyed wearing a Red Army uniform, visited nursery schools and other Moscow institutions named after him, and basked in the flattery that the pro-Stalin Russians heaped upon him. He revelled in his standing as 'the revolutionary German worker' and as an anti-militarist, he positively enjoyed leading the Rotfrontkämpferbund (the Fighters for the Red Front).

Then, in an astonishingly theatrical gesture, he flung himself into the presidential elections of 1925. The election was won by the aged, still venerated Hindenburg, but it gave Germany's Communists a new, nationwide respectability.

Thälmann at the hustings was something the Germans had not quite encountered before. He would 'play' the crowds who listened to him, often drawing on deep-felt emotions, declaiming at the top of his voice. If the occasion was right, he would tear off his white collar. It was all a far cry from the relative gentility of Paul Levi (or Marx, Engels and Liebknecht for that matter) and it meant that a Thälmann legend was born. This legend is perpetuated to this day, though the fact that he was a Stalin creation — and would certainly have got nowhere without his patronage — is hardly mentioned.

Whatever mechanism it was that kept Thälmann's star in the ascendant began to falter in the late 1920s. There was a move to have him removed from the KPD Central Committee which at first seemed to succeed. Stalin was outraged and had him reinstated, purging the Right immediately afterwards for its 'error'.

Thälmann's success as a demagogue and his uncanny ability to foresee the horrors of Nazism before they happened made him a natural target for the Nazis. He was one of the first to be arrested in the aftermath of the stage-managed Reichstag fire of 1933, and he died at Buchenwald concentration camp in 1944. Today he is remembered in East Berlin with one of the city's biggest statues (bigger than Lenin, Marx or Engels) and a large park and housing estate. He is never criticised.

Two others who never lost Stalin's favour on the German scene were Wilhelm Pieck and Walter Ulbricht. In the twilight years of the Weimar Republic these two men, with Thälmann, did much to reorganise the KPD, shaping it along 'correct' lines into an organism of which Stalin approved and parts of which he was to nurse carefully during the Second World War so that, once the formalities with the other big powers were completed, they could take over in a new Communist Germany. In Fischer's account, Pieck and Ulbricht 'smashed' the German party. They would have achieved nothing without Stalin's secret police.

Pieck was by all accounts a genial man — a joiner by trade — born in Frankfurt-on-Oder and growing up in Bremen. He was a Communist of the old school who had worked closely with Rosa Luxemburg in the last ten years of her life. He was even arrested with her and Liebknecht, but since there was no substantial price on his head, he was released. From what is known of KPD activities after these two died, he might have been willing to reach an accommodation, even in the early 1920s, with the SPD (something which was finally achieved in 1946). He was at times less than happy at Soviet 'interference' in German affairs though his son was to become a Soviet Army officer. Of tangential interest is that he wanted the much respected Clara Zetkin to stand for president against Hindenburg rather than Thälmann, but was overruled.

Walter Ulbricht was, like Pieck, a joiner by trade. His political initiation was as an agitator in Leipzig before the First World War, distributing pamphlets in the streets for the SPD. His end came in East Berlin, proclaimed capital of the GDR, where he had been undisputed leader for more than twenty-five years. In the Liebknecht Museum in Leipzig, there is a picture of him as a boy of fifteen, a member of a youth group. He was born in Gottsched-strasse, not far from the city centre, a tired and gap-toothed street of tenement blocks. A plain, dusty plaque, just above eye level on the wall of one of these blocks, confirms the fact of his birth.

Ulbricht, whom I studied over a number of years and watched at several public functions, remains a puzzling, inscrutable figure, a committed Communist all his life, but hardly a spontaneous and compassionate champion of the people as Rosa Luxemburg and, in a different way, Thälmann, were. He was a devious man with little sense of honour, a prodigious memory, and a certain capacity for organisation. He was more important for what he became — East Germany's chief defender and head of state, and a major influence on the European stage — than for the sort of human being, or political animal, that he was, which was a cautious, usually centrist political schemer.

In 1918-1919, he had fought for the party at the Leipzig barricades, and after the débâcle of 1923, had begun to be noticed as an ambitious, if somewhat colourless, organiser, often in Thälmann's proximity. For the last five years of the Weimar Republic, he was a KPD deputy in the Reichstag, for much of the time also party organiser for the Berlin district.

When the Nazis came to power Ulbricht, like Pieck and many others, left the country, dividing his time between France, Czechoslovakia, the Soviet Union and Spain. Like so many of the exiles, he was dependent on Soviet philanthropy to stay alive. For much of the Second World War he was in or near the Soviet capital, a leading light in the Committees for a 'Free Germany'. He and Pieck were among a small handful, to become known as the Ulbricht group, who arrived in a devastated Berlin, setting up an institutional framework for the running of the city in the crucial weeks before the Americans arrived. They and others who gathered round them were consistently at pains to buttress Stalin's concern, which dated from the mid-1920s, that the Soviet Union needed defending, and that Germany was the front line of that defence. Soviet 'interference' was no longer a public issue.

When Hitler assumed control in early 1933, the Communists — by then the biggest party outside the Soviet Union — were inevitably his prime target. It mattered little that only a few months before Nazis and Communists had stood together in a transport strike, that both parties were acutely concerned by dangerously high unemployment and falling living standards, or that there were more than eighty KPD members of the Reichstag. Hitler had already shown by his writings and by his actions that he would be a more or less fanatical anti-Communist all his political life.

In the twelve years of Nazi control over Germany, the Communist struggle was characterised by resistance either from underground or from beyond Germany's frontiers. Often the resistance was pointless, but often it was a matter of great personal and political courage in the face of constant danger, infiltration, hardship and stress. The Communists had no power base in the army or the police (where the Nazis were increasingly dominant) and had no formal overground organisation, but somehow the struggle continued with an effectiveness that was savagely confirmed by the Nazis' reprisals against it.

An enduring hatred for the Nazis and what they did to Germany, and to Germany's Communists especially, complicated by a guilt which an unknown number of Germans (on both sides) must feel about their role and their parents' role in the Nazi period, continues to be one of the chief justifications for the Socialist Unity Party (SED), as the ruling party calls itself,* having power in East Germany today. Any political speech which touches on history is invariably contemptuous towards the Nazis and enthusiastic about the KPD and what it did during Nazi rule. But some unexpected allies have been uncovered. The Junker class, because it was dominant in the July 1944 plot against the Führer, is now accorded some praise.

During the panic years which followed the Wall Street crash and which just preceded Hitler's takeover, there had been a surge in KPD membership — up to 360,000 by the beginning of 1933. Many of the membership were young and many belonged to the working class; a large proportion were unemployed. In the late 1932 elections, shortly before Hitler's moment came, the KPD had taken nearly 38 per cent of the votes, half as many again as the SPD. Returns were such that many of the Communists grew dizzily unrealistic about the strength of the Nazis, and once again there were calls for immediate revolution.

The Reichstag fire, and the trumped-up charges which followed, buried these hopes for many. The fire was blamed unequivocally on the Communists — Josef Goebbels, as Berlin's

*The SED, as will be clarified in a later chapter, is the result of an amalgamation — in 1946 — of the Communist Party (the KPD) and the Social Democrats (the SPD).

Gauleiter, was very specific on this — and around 10,000 party members were rounded up the following day, 1500 of them in Berlin. A leading Communist, the Bulgarian Georgi Dimitrov, was one of several tried for starting the fire and an unknown number left Germany as quickly as they could. The party was once again outlawed. It is astonishing that against such a background of retribution and repression, in elections held just six days after the fire, the Communists could still win nearly five million votes. By the end of the year, however, there were about 130,000 Communists — more than a third of the membership — in concentration camps. About 1500 had been murdered, often after torture.

The party, though underground, kept its message in the public eye. There were two leaderships: one 'inland' and still on German soil (which for a while included Ulbricht) and the second overseas (which included Pieck). As ever, there were factional disputes but there were increasing calls for discipline and unity. One way of achieving this was through activities reminiscent of those pursued half a century before by the proscribed SPD: there was a sudden increase in the number of (non-Nazi) educational meetings and organised weekend walks, children's parties, and so on. At the very least it was a character-forming period, and a time when many of those most committed party veterans whom I have met in East Germany won their spurs.

A real difficulty for the KPD was what can only be described as the 'success' of Nazi politics in important areas. Unemployment did fall sharply, nationalism did induce a sense of common purpose, and foreign policy initiatives did seem to go well. However, Dimitrov, once exculpated by the court, rallied both the outlawed party and the trade unionists, which had also been disbanded, and tried to persuade the workers to unite more effectively. Pieck and Ulbricht, despite opposition from the party's own executive and from grassroots activists, agitated to unite the Left into some sort of popular front.

Driven to carry on the struggle and to defend themselves on the slenderest of resources and only minimal chances of popular acceptance, the party's most important support, from the men, money and morale point of view, had to come from Stalin and the Soviet Union. This was in spite of the fact that, as history has shown — though not yet very graphically to the East German people — the Soviet leader had other serious preoccupations in that period. His determination to develop socialism in one country, or so it had seemed, had led to an unprecedented purge of the Soviet party to clear out real and (often) imagined opposition. This was the time of the 'great terror'.

Other parties, including the KPD, conducted their own ruthless cleansing operations. Stalin's henchmen purged or persecuted Germans inside the Soviet Union who were not 'ideologically sound'. Ulbricht, it is now said, was active in Spain during the civil war there, imprisoning and even authorising the torture of hundreds of Trotskyists and other German 'dissidents'.

When Stalin concluded a non-aggression treaty with Hitler shortly before the global war got under way, party members at home were stunned. Some even committed suicide, even though in the years before this act was perpetrated, and as the war progressed and Europe was overrun, Moscow was to remain the most sought-after port in the storm.

Other German groups came into being in Paris, Prague and other centres beyond Germany's frontiers. Defiant groups still inside the country continued to operate clandestine printing presses, to hold clandestine meetings and to distribute exhortatory pamphlets wherever and whenever they could. The resistance has become legendary of Communists, pacifists and other supporters, like Carl von Ossietzky who spoke up for the intellectuals, of Herbert von Baum and his wife who represented Jewish interests, or a young printer called Heinz Kapelle.

As the war progressed, the Moscow-based group slipped into the leadership role, drawing together the German refugees who were living in the Soviet Union and Soviet-held prisoners-of-war to increase their numbers. The old-fashioned Hotel Lux, in Moscow, overrun with bugs, rats and members of the GPU (forerunners of the KGB), was their headquarters. It was a place where ordinary Russians were not allowed to tread. KPD meetings in this hotel, and occasionally in the Kremlin, gained in importance as more and more Communists were rounded up back home.

An important turning point was reached when Ulbricht went to a prison camp for Germans at Krasnogorsk, near the Soviet capital, in October 1941, where he outlined plans for a Communist Germany. He then went on to hold other meetings with captive audiences elsewhere. Moscow's orchestration of Germany's future had begun in earnest. By the time Ulbricht went to the front line, including Stalingrad, to address advancing Nazi troops through a megaphone, and when Stalingrad was finally re-taken by the Russians in the spring of 1943, that process became irreversible.

It was in the summer of 1943, at another key meeting near Moscow, that the 'National Committee for a Free Germany' was formally established. Ulbricht and Pieck, now joined by Anton Ackermann, a working-class intellectual who had been active in the party in Berlin in the early 1930s, were at its centre. A broad brushstroke manifesto and agreements of understanding were signed with political officials of the Soviet Army. The war still had two years to run.

Within six months, another committee was set up — led by Pieck — to determine KPD priorities in Germany once Hitler was defeated. This body led to plans being formulated in early 1944 to take over the German economy, including agriculture and the trade unions, and to establish a 'new' relationship with the Soviet Union. In principle, the plans were for the whole of Germany, though of course they were not to be realised in that form. What was important at this stage, however, was that the experience of adversity during the war, coupled with the insistent tutoring from their Soviet mentors, had given German Communists in exile an unprecedented sense of unity and purpose and an agreed path to follow.

Third Excursion: Trauma in Dresden

Dresden is not what it was. Fewer and fewer people remain who can still visualise its one-time glories from personal memory. It is a city now with vestiges of greatness only, where, as elsewhere in East Germany, there have been valiant efforts to retrieve what was lost but where the austere geometry of the present is a poor complement to the sensitive, refurbished lines of the past.

The rebuilders have the best of intentions, no doubt — and I have met several of them — and they have notched up a number of clear successes. But they can only go as far as their own, and their masters', limitations allow. In the modern East European society, the present and the future, rather than the niceties of the past, are always with us.

It was in February 1945 that Dresden was bombed — just a couple of days after Stalin had completed his act as host at Yalta to Britain's Winston Churchill and the ailing US President Roosevelt for talks on the already imminent 'final defeat' of Germany. In a savage coup de grâce which was to become one of the most notorious acts of the entire war, the spirit of a superb city, which perhaps more than any other could be seen as bringing together the threads of the country's cultural history, was destroyed.

No one agrees on how many died in those traumatic visitations by British and American aircraft. Figures vary between 35,000 and 135,000. However, they are remembered, especially at convenient anniversaries, and have given the East German authorities opportunities to exploit their own needs and demands for peace in our time. Meanwhile, from all shades of the political spectrum, there are those who declare that the bombing need not, should not, have happened when it did and that the many thousands need not have died.

Hitler's Propaganda Minister, Josef Goebbels, was said to be devastated when he heard of the city's destruction. Tears of grief, rage and shock came into his eyes. Not long after, his personal assistant wrote: 'He looked like a broken man, but then came a passionate outburst of rage. His veins swelled and he became as red as a lobster . . . .'

To that extent the bombing raid may be adjudged to have been a success. A jewel of the European Renaissance, baroque architecture and urban 'style' was consumed in one of the biggest fire-storms the world had yet seen. Present-day visitors can be reduced to a poignant perambulation through disturbing spaces among the salvaged architectural gems which now stand in splendid isolation one from the other. The colour of what has been salvaged contrasts with the disturbing blackness of the untouched. Somehow the welcome is not complete, but it is not the fault of those who live there.

Tourists from both parts of Europe — searching perhaps for another inkling of their inheritance — flock to the city in their hundreds of thousands every year. One of East Germany's most sumptuous hotels, the Belle Vue, has recently been built on the site of what used to be one of Dresden's oldest and most picturesque districts, on the north bank of the Elbe facing the Altstadt. Its earnings are a significant contributor to East Germany's hard currency reserves, but the 'ordinary' people of Dresden have little to do with it.

Dresden's finest times were in the eighteenth century. A visiting poet described the city then as 'the Florence of Germany'. Within living memory it was the royal capital of Saxony, but its very best of times as a capital was the period of August the Strong. He was mainly responsible for a skyline which, according to Kurt Vonnegut in *Slaughterhouse Five*, was simultaneously 'intricate and voluptuous and enchanted and absurd'.

Today, the King is back, on his horse and lovingly regilded, on a high pedestal in the city centre. The Zwinger gallery, built to his orders in about 1710 around a variety of fountains and ornamental gardens to house some of the then world's greatest art, has been rebuilt. So have the cathedral nearby, the royal mews, and other residences, pavilions, terraces and parks of the period. In 1985, forty years on from the fateful bombardment, the Semper Opera House — 90 per cent destroyed but with much of its old glitter restored — reopened with a gala performance of Weber's opera, *Der Freischütz*.

Once, the centre of the city must have had a unity and harmony of the sort more readily associated with, for instance, the centre of Edinburgh or the city of Cambridge. But even before the First World War, great tracts of medieval domestic architecture, which lined so many narrow streets, had been cleared away by ambitious city planners. In the Nazi era, the city was earmarked to become a light industrial centre and the biggest military garrison in the Third Reich. Then in the February raids of 1945, several square miles of it were completely destroyed.

My first visit to Dresden was not auspicious. I had come from Prague on a summer's evening, a visually magical experience, following a line along the side of the Elbe through the eastern end of the Erzgebirge mountains that separate the two Germanies from Czechoslovakia. The understanding, reached with the East German Embassy in London before my departure, was that my entry visa would be no problem. The frontier guards on the train would expect me, stamp my passport and nod me through.

They did not expect me, and when the train reached Dresden, three of us disembarked — myself with a uniformed frontier guard on either side of me. We walked the length of what seemed a very long platform. My passport was taken from me, and I was locked up for an hour and a half in a windowless room.

In this cell the magic of the journey evaporated very quickly. Even though I knew I had done nothing illegal, I vacillated between telling myself that everything would be all right and breaking out into an uncomfortable sweat. I finished up in an uneasy state of suspended animation which was somewhere between the two.

At length, as my reasonable self had expected, the passport came back duly stamped. I was dismissed into the night. Having found a hotel of suitable substance, I booked myself into a room and prepared for bed. Towards midnight there was an agitated telephone call. 'Mr Simmons? My name is Rüdiger M. and I am to meet you. I am sorry I did not meet you. Are you all right? Welcome to the GDR.'

As the embarrassed sentences tumbled down the line, I realised that if I had contemplated panic, Rüdiger was actually living it. I told him to relax and said I would join him downstairs for a drink in ten minutes.

After three beers he had calmed down enough to accept my assurances that I would not 'shop' him if he promised not to pass on any of the awkward questions I might ply him with on the week's tour of the GDR we were about to undertake together. He agreed, and we have been good friends ever since.

My second landing in the city also had its disconcerting moments. It was winter and bitterly cold. My appointed interpreter and appointed driver had just completed with me the hundred miles or so south from Berlin along a dreary autobahn, and had reached Dresden — which the guidebook described as the centre-piece of 'a pleasant valley of the Elbe' — at lunchtime. We were hungry and decided to eat. But everywhere we tried to find a table, there was none available. The bigger restaurants were either closed or had long queues at the door.

We finished up in an enormous Orwellian eating hall queuing to serve ourselves to a cheap dish of fritters and sloshy mash with a glass of anaemic fruit juice. Then we realised that the dozens of stone-topped tables, each with eight or ten fixed chairs along its sides, were also busy, or had been. Dirty plates and bits of food, uneaten or inedible, littered their surfaces, awaiting a non-existent cleaner with cloth. Sullen 'workers', or grandparents with small children, ate silently. There were hundreds of men and women in the room, as there probably are every working day of the week, but the main sounds were the clatter of dishes and trays. My companions felt constrained to apologise even though, presumably, this was a routine environment for them to find themselves in. It was another facet of this European jewel.

The city's historians have chosen their words with care. 'At a time when it was already established that Dresden would be in the Soviet occupation zone,' says my guide book of 1970, 'Anglo-American squadrons bombed the city on 13 and 14 February 1945, without the slighest military necessity for this action. The Soviet Army was intended to take over a dead city.'

'The intention,' says a slightly more moderate guidebook of 1983, 'was to leave a sea of ruins for the Soviet troops.'

Dresden burned easily. Large areas of housing were made mainly of wood. Of the total of 220,000 homes, an estimated 75,000 to 80,000 were totally destroyed, and only 45,000 escaped damage. More than a quarter of a million people, according to official East German statistics, were made homeless. But that figure is contentious. Every open space on those winter nights of the bombing was filled with refugees living, or rather surviving, in the most wretched of conditions. Many had come to the city from points to the east, where advancing Soviet troops were wreaking revenge, often indiscriminately, for the horrors their own people had gone through at the hands of the Nazis not so long before.

At No. 46 Industriestrasse, I went to see Frau Erna Lange. In the cluttered sitting room of her cramped but spotlessly tidy flat, she remembered the night of the firestorm.

'My mother sat in the basement, holding her hands to her ears,' she said over tea and cakes. 'She was very frightened. We lived on the outskirts and I cycled into town to see my cousin. Everything was burning. We were told to come back the next day.

'When we did, everything was gone. The stones of the street were too hot to walk on and yet you could hear screams from the cellars. We couldn't do anything. A lot of people were very dirty and their faces had a very strange look. They pushed little carts with their belongings in.'

She recalled the trams, welded by the heat to their rails, with their passengers still aboard, men still wearing their hats, women their headscarves. The inside of their lungs had burned, but they had not.

She also recalled looking for a friend who lived near the Kreuzkirche on the Old Market Square, but found the church and the square virtually unrecognisable 'There were soldiers with rubber aprons,' she said. 'They were carrying bodies about in tin baths. They had had a drink or two to fortify themselves and I could understand that.'

After the second raid, which was totally unexpected, Erna told me, the fire burned out of control for five days and nights. There was nobody to control it. It took six years to clear the rubble and the mess from the part of Dresden where her cousin lived. Great pyres to burn the recovered bodies were lit after ten days. Erna was to find no trace at all of her cousin or of her four children.

Forty years on, in the basement of Dresden City Hall, I met the chief architect. A room about the size of a tennis court was filled with models of the city. Some were of the city that was, others of how the city should look, and still others of how it almost certainly will look, when the first phase of rebuilding, which ends in the year 2000, is complete. His task has not been helped by the fact that many of the original plans were lost in the fire, and that a number of the surviving city fathers were all in favour of rebuilding from scratch in another part of Germany.

Alfred Althus, who lived in the centre of Dresden in the Weisse Gasse, was already over seventy when I met him, but he gave a vivid description of watching his own house burn down that February night from a vantage point on the opposite river bank by the old Japanese Palace, a spot now subsumed by the Karl–Marx–Platz.

That was on the second night. After the first, he had left his house with a rucksack of belongings, the house having been blitzed so badly that it was barely habitable. After he had watched it burn down, he and his sister set off to find their mother at a place to which she had retreated in the country. They reached her in time to celebrate her fifty-eighth birthday. 'We were her birthday present,' he said. '*Aber Dresden war ein riesiges Trümmerfeld.*' ('Dresden was one huge stretch of rubble.')

Alfred was an old SPD man. He said that after the bombing, his cell of the SPD joined forces with the Communists to fight on against Hitler. They got their moral support, he said, from J.B. Priestley's broadcasts which they heard illegally on the radio. Erna joined the Communist Party in 1945 and has been, she said, a member ever since. It was terrible, she added, that 'even after Dresden', Hitler would not give in.

Both of these survivors were chosen for me by the press liaison authorities in East Berlin. Clearly, the accounts they gave me were well-rehearsed and had been delivered many times. But they both differed in very acceptable ways from the guide book and the museum coldness, and that was welcome.

Ten weeks after the destruction of Dresden, and only a matter of days before the end of the war, Soviet and American troops met on a bridge crossing the Elbe, close to the little town of Torgau, about forty-five miles to the north-west of Dresden. It was the signal for the Moscow-based National Committee for Free Germany under Walter Ulbricht, to act. They prepared to fly into Berlin. 'This was the first time,' wrote one of the immediate team, 'that I had ever seen him smiling and friendly.'

The Soviet Zone

In the spring of 1945, the German people came out of what one veteran Communist has graphically called 'the darkest night in German history'. Six million of them had died, twenty-five million were refugees, and a third of the national product was destroyed. The future, it seemed, would be dominated indefinitely by endless talk of atonement, years of insurmountable guilt and other psychological uncertainties. Countless millions were to be paid in reparations.

A new generation, like the one that preceded it, had been defeated in war. Many homes remained intact, but in cities and towns living was reduced to unpredictable wretchedness. Whole families, or what remained of whole families, endured and improvised in little more than holes in the ground, or in cellars where the weight of rubble above meant the ceiling could cave in any minute. Everywhere there was overcrowding. But a roof was a roof. To keep alive, many were reduced to scavenging, begging, or prostitution. Others exploited the black market.

Andrei Gromyko, though still in his thirties, was Soviet Ambassador to the United States. He was in Berlin with Stalin's team for the Potsdam summit on post-war Europe. 'We observed the ruined capital of Hitler's reich,' he wrote, 'and there were precious few undamaged or even half-destroyed buildings to be seen. Only some of the smaller houses in the outlying districts remained unscathed. I remember the difficulty our jeep had in negotiating Unter den Linden, littered as it was along its entire length by collapsed walls. There were bricks, mountains of bricks, everywhere.'

At such a desolate and inauspicious time, two contrasting

groups of Communists wanted to influence events: those who had stuck it out on the home front since 1933, and those who in slightly easier circumstances had suffered in exile. It is not surprising that their representatives failed to see eye to eye.

The vanguard of those who now came out on top had been delivered to the fatherland in Soviet aircraft or lorries, complying with instructions from the Soviet military occupation forces and subsisting initially on roubles and other resources that were provided by them. Ostensibly led by Walter Ulbricht, Anton Ackermann, Franz Dahlem and others, these were to be the new helmsmen of Germany. The 'home front' residue of the old Communist Party were to make up the crew.

Although Stalin was to make some disingenuous moves to take over the whole of Germany for Communism, backed on a number of occasions by unambiguous speeches from Walter Ulbricht, it was to be in the Soviet zone of occupation that these Communists consolidated their hold. The frontiers have changed very little since 1945. The fight to take the zone and keep it as the Soviet area of influence began inside Russia long before the war ended — even before the war began. To understand politics in East Germany, the way in which that particular fight was fought has to be looked at.

The nucleus of the so-called Ulbricht Group which arrived in Germany a few days before the actual ending of hostilities was just ten strong. It came under the banner of the National Committee for a Free Germany. Ulbricht was at its head because, during the war years, he had managed to achieve a special and apparently close relationship with the Soviet generals most involved in the assault on Berlin. He and the members of the Soviet-based 'Committee' had been groomed for power under Stalin's auspices.

This grooming was a process which had taken place in conditions of stringent secrecy and exclusivity, in an environment of privilege and status. But Stalin's purges of 'Trotskyites and traitors' during the 1930s and beyond had not excluded the newly arrived German community. While close relatives were savagely separated for inexplicable reasons, those who were earmarked to be part of the post-war zone's Supreme Political Administration lived a life which in the deprived war years was astonishingly comfortable in the circumstances.

In the streets outside the centres where they were being fed and housed, and primed to take their part in the Ulbricht Group, there was poverty, and even destitution among local Soviet citizens. Wolfgang Leonhard, who spent ten years in the Soviet Union before joining Ulbricht in the 1945 takeover, has left a graphic account of that unreality. He found it disconcerting.

By the mid-1930s, several thousand Germans had converged on Moscow, effectively reversing the process which had sent waves of Russians into Berlin ten years before. The displaced Germans were mainly Communist and they formed their own social networks. In doing so, they soon learned that the Soviet Union was not necessarily the promised land.

Soviet authorities took upon themselves powers to approve, and to censor what Germans could read — banning books and blacking out passages in publications deemed unsafe. They prescribed the content and much of the 'tone' of the instruction given in notionally German teaching establishments. When the otherwise unexpected Soviet-Nazi non-aggression treaty was signed in 1939, Germans who were in the Soviet Union and who wanted to prosper became vocal in their support. When, for nearly two years as a result of that treaty, Hitler's every act was met with daily Soviet approval, Soviet-based Germans had to agree. When Stalin was pronounced infallible, they sang his praises.

When rumours of an imminent invasion by Hitler reached fever-pitch in mid-1941, Soviet newspapers declared them to be 'pure fantasy'. Days later, the Nazi attack began. With this event, the seeds of the GDR as we know it were sown.

The Comintern's headquarters from the autumn of 1941 were at Ufa, 750 miles east of Moscow, almost in the Ural mountains. Here, with Pieck and Ulbricht among the luminaries, and at a 'school' in Kushnarenkovo, forty miles further to the north-west, German cadres were prepared. Leaving the premises without permission was prohibited, as were close friendships with the opposite sex. No one used their own name and no one publicly discussed themes which had dominated German political life, and especially the evolution of the Communist Party, only a few years before. Recent history, in other words, was heavily doctored.

Soviet-authorised propaganda was intense. There were

megaphone addresses to Nazi troops on the front line (notably in the long battle for Stalingrad) and there were highly charged political speeches to German prisoners-of-war. The German People's Radio station beamed a regular message into a beleaguered Third Reich. When, after 1943, Stalingrad was retaken and the war changed course, the propaganda increased — becoming if anything more one-sided.

By the end of 1944, dozens of Nazi generals who had been taken prisoner by the Russians joined the Free Germany movement. 'Free Germans' began talking in broadcasts of 'the richly deserved destruction of Hitlerite Germany' which was then getting under way. By that time, a group had formed around Ulbricht, but he was 'rather unsympathetic', according to Leonhard, who said that he was 'ruthless' and 'skilful' in carrying out orders, and capable of behaving 'like a dictator'.

The decisive move to Berlin was made at the end of April 1945. In the confusion which saw Hitler commit suicide and the Soviet Army close in on Berlin, and then the final surrender, the Ulbricht group moved resolutely ahead. Once installed, Soviet officers and their German henchmen recruited known and self-proclaimed 'anti-fascists' to become Mayors and to form malleable local authority administrations. In Dresden, where the more imaginative Anton Ackermann was the controlling German, the prime organisation was called the Anti-Fascist People's Committee. But when it was found that only about one in four of its membership were actually Communists, the organisation fell apart. Many, in Leonhard's words, withdrew in disappointment to private life. 'Every initiative from below,' he noted heavily, 'was nipped in the bud.'

The new Supreme Political Administration under Ulbricht behaved in a frequently ad hoc way to establish its authority, sometimes going dramatically against plans worked out in Moscow not so many months before. Thus, when Marshal Georgi Zhukov, military leader of the Soviet occupation forces (the SMAD), decreed that 'democratic anti-fascist parties' and trade unions should be permitted to exist, the machinery was set in motion to allow this to happen. But it was done in direct contradiction to plans made in Moscow.

The authorities in Moscow — guided by Stalin — provided the text for the first proclamation of the post-war Communist Party. It was read out by Ulbricht to a meeting of about eighty party stalwarts, many of whom had been recruited in the few weeks since the war ended. There were some surprising elements.

'We take the view,' it said, 'that the method of imposing the Soviet system on Germany would be wrong, since this method does not correspond to present-day conditions of development in Germany. We take the view rather that the overriding interests of the German people in their present-day situation prescribe a different method for Germany, namely the method of establishing a democratic anti-fascist regime, a parliamentary democratic republic with full democratic rights and liberties.'

If this message jolted dyed-in-the-wool Communists who were present, so did the smaller print. This envisaged the 'complete and unrestricted' development of free enterprise, democratic rights and civil liberties, self-governing democratic institutions, and it included clauses which recognised the need for land reform and obligations to pay reparations.

Only marginally less bewildering was the announcement a little later from Ulbricht himself that 'we are forming a party of a new type'. When he was asked how his programme varied from that of any other recently formed democratic party, he merely replied: 'Wait and see.' When a voice from the floor demanded that Socialism be established in Germany 'without and, if necessary, against the Red Army', it was ignored.

Weeding out Nazis was one of the first and most formidable undertakings. After the war, according to East German figures, a total of 16,572 persons were tried for Nazi and other war crimes. Four out of five of these were convicted, with 118 sentenced to death and nearly twice as many given life imprisonment. More than 5000 were sent to prison for three years or more.

By a variety of processes, thousands lost their jobs. Sometimes it was done semi-formally, with a semblance of ceremony; sometimes, ex-Nazis were chased off the premises where they worked. Professionals deemed to have been active Hitler supporters were given manual work, often on rebuilding sites. Hundred of judges and thousands of teachers were 're-trained' for other employment. It was as if the 'little man' of the 1920s was at last getting his revenge for old social and other injustices.

But if in the 1920s the 'little man' was a natural ally of the then Communists, his political allegiance twenty years later was not so clear. In late 1945, Ackermann promulgated his ideas for 'a separate German road to socialism', pointing out as he did so that conditions in Germany were, despite the war and the reparations now demanded, more propitious than they had been in Russia in 1917. Germany had a more developed and more numerous working class — better equipped than even Karl Marx might have anticipated, and a 'peaceful transition' was therefore feasible.

Intellectually, it was an attractive proposition, but it had little appeal for Ulbricht because it took too little account of Soviet paymasters, and after a few years on the back-burner it sputtered out and died. Ackermann himself faded out a little later.

These developments, of course, were ones about which the man and woman in the street knew or cared little. Materially, they were still surviving in very reduced circumstances, with deprivation and shortages their main concern rather than the niceties of politics. Their prime concern was to rebuild something akin to self-respect.

While Ackermann's ideas were still fresh, however, wheels were set in motion to amalgamate the Social Democrats and the Communists to form a single new party. In a colourful ceremony, with flowers and flags, an orchestra playing Beethoven and homage being paid to the long-dead August Bebel, this amalgamation duly happened.

Ulbricht, on this occasion, did not push himself too far forward. Wilhelm Pieck, his warmer and more experienced colleague, was the one who symbolically shook hands with the SPD leader, Otto Grotewohl. No matter that hundreds, possibly thousands, of SPD members had to be shipped out of Berlin to allow the ceremony to go through without obvious complications. This was the birth of Sozialistische Einheitspartei Deutschlands (SED). It is this Party which rules the GDR today.

Attempts to force through the implementation of new policies lacked subtlety. The programming of industrial production in the strictly national interest was very complicated, as were the proposals for thorough-going land reform. These were given effect as estates of more than 250 acres, or those which had once belonged to known Nazis, were taken over, either to become state farms or to be divided up into plots for smallholders. Not until 1960, the era of Nikita Khrushchev in Moscow, was collectivisation to be enforced on a much bigger scale.

Changes of this nature were usually unhindered. For the majority, day-to-day survival was what mattered most. Obtaining enough to eat, the wherewithal to keep warm, to make a home, however battered, more like a home, were still of more importance and more time-consuming than the niceties of 'new type' socialism and the single-minded intentions of Walter Ulbricht. Bargains on the black market were what gave badly needed boosts to morale.

Reparations were an issue that Ulbricht refused to discuss even with unhappy Communists, and his continued truculence in the face of questions did nothing to enhance his own standing, as a figure admired but not liked, or the wider popularity of his party. Hundreds of plants were removed, engineering workshops and mining installations were dismantled, mile after mile of railway lines were ripped up and taken away. Many of the Soviet zone's biggest manufacturers – in chemicals, machine-making and shipbuilding, for example – watched as their production was loaded up and exported, for no return at all, to the Soviet Union. This process went on until the beginning of 1954.

Attitudes to the Russians, and to Soviet power, coloured whatever contact there was between people living in the zone and those thousands who were coming into the zone as refugees. They had been flowing almost non-stop since the Red Army first crossed onto German soil in the drive for Berlin. Until the Soviet military authorities tightened their regulations governing the troops' behaviour, there were endless, and only occasionally exaggerated, tales about the rapes and rapaciousness of some of the Soviet troops. Added to this, there was also speculation over the fate of the missing Germans – men who were either prisoners in Soviet camps or who, for whatever reason, had not been traced once the fighting ceased on the eastern front.

In such circumstances there was little revolutionary zeal in the air. Ulbricht was a highly effective executive of Soviet-approved policy; but he was not someone the people in the streets wanted to follow to the barricades. For many Germans, he was a person without charisma, and because of things he could not help — such as a squeaky voice and a goatee beard — he was a figure of fun.

These drawbacks notwithstanding, it was this man who ordered East Germans to take the road to Communism. Karl Marx, for all his faults, was a human being, as was Friedrich Engels. A hundred years on from their manifesto of 1848, they might well have winced. Ulbricht was hardly the sort of person they would have regarded as a revolutionary trail-blazer.

External developments played into Ulbricht's hands. In western Germany and Berlin, British and American occupiers moved closer together, creating an entity called Bizonia as an economic unit. In the spring of 1948, disagreements in the three-power Control Council in Berlin now led to the abrupt walk-out of the Soviet delegation, under Marshal Vassily Sokolowski, since — according to him — the council had lost its overall authority in the defeated country.

An economic blockade of West Berlin was instituted by the Russians. It ran from late June 1948, for almost eleven months. West Berlin, through the much-trumpeted airlifting of emergency food and fuel supplies, survived and was strengthened. East Berlin, and Eastern Germany, also survived, but were weakened in the sense that they had now moved beyond arm's length as far as international credibility and acceptability were concerned.

In 1948 Josip Broz Tito, the Yugoslav partisan leader, who had 'come to socialism' by a totally different route from that which had been followed by the Germans, was suddenly declared to be a traitor and Trotskyite. His defiance of Stalin, and his wilful independence in foreign policy, have gone down in history. There were many party loyalists in Germany who approved of Tito's line. All they could do was swallow that approval and forget about it.

Once again, it was an issue Ulbricht declined to discuss openly. Democratic centralism, by which the agreed party line remains agreed, meant that pro-Tito loyalists either had to leave the party or to keep silent. A purge was launched. It led to the expulsion of more than 150,000 party members.

Irreconcilable formulations were being advanced meanwhile to solve 'the German question'. West German dissatisfaction with what was happening in the East grew as the blockade of West Berlin continued, fuelled by sabre-rattling Allied generals as well as the recalcitrant Stalin and Ulbricht. But the emergence of the equally single-minded Konrad Adenauer, a staunch Conservative former Lord Mayor of Cologne who was a wayward federalist by persuasion, meant these two had met their match.

Adenauer's leadership of a Parliamentary Council in Bonn, a location very much of his choosing, led to approval of the Basic Law and the establishment, in May 1949, of the Federal Republic of Germany. The North Atlantic Treaty Organisation was born at much the same time.

Within a few weeks, a People's Council was set up in East Berlin. Its members voted in October to reconstitute themselves as a People's Assembly, and by the evening of the same day this body had endorsed the birth of the German Democratic Republic. Otto Grotewohl, the old SPD member of the Reichstag, was asked to form the GDR's first Government and Wilhelm Pieck, the seventy-three-year old former joiner with impeccable Communist credentials, became president.

The country now born had come after a gestation period which had lasted several years. The real father's name was unclear, but there was no shortage of godfathers. When celebrations were held in the heart of Berlin, with processions along Unter den Linden, there was plenty of competition for places on the saluting platform.

The birth of two new states on German soil did nothing to stem the flow of proposals for a unified Germany. Stalin's message to a foreign ministers' meeting in Paris, in May 1949, that all occupation forces should be withdrawn and a neutral Germany should be created, was returned to sender. A note was added to the effect that if such a Germany were formed there should be a multi-lateral high commission, taking decisions by a majority vote, to see it through.

Both proposals were left hanging in the air, though even in his last years Stalin went on calling for a neutralised Germany, as did his successor, Nikita Khrushchev, in the years that followed. Now the likelihood of such a demand coming out of Moscow has receded out of sight, and it is the West Germans who call the tune.

Germany's new Communists did what they could do to assure

the standing of the new regime. They arranged small briefing groups and convened meetings, for which all work was usually stopped, in factories, offices and farms throughout the country. The word 'discipline', and the evident need for it, began to figure in political speeches. It still figures today. The spectre of Communism, which had been spotted by a couple of exiled Germans as haunting Europe a hundred years before, was now made flesh. A Prussian uniform, it seemed, was part of its wardrobe.

Party membership when the GDR came into being stood at about 1.3 million, but its leadership was not happy that old SPD loyalties still flickered. The 'bourgeois' influence, it thought, was still virulent. Over a period of months, nearly 70,000 party members were purged — often, it was later acknowledged, for the wrong reasons. But the Party's 'leading role' had to be asserted.

Consolidation meant seeking to involve more people in party and state decision-making. Ulbricht spoke of 'building' socialism in East Germany. It was a process in which the newly authorised trade unions acquiesced, but rank-and-file workers had their doubts. There was a nagging feeling on the factory floor that the workers once again were being exploited; on the land, there was outright resistance to collectivisation. The drift westwards of individuals who wanted no part in the process began to increase perceptibly. Everyone who voted with their feet was a source of alarm to the authorities.

In 1951, when the first five-year plan got under way, nearly a third of all industrial output was from Soviet-run enterprises. When Stalin died in 1953, an important prop to the regime's legitimacy was removed. Because living and working conditions for the majority were still far from satisfactory, and because food was still short (and the farmers were not wholly co-operating), morale in the country remained low.

Radical changes were needed in policy-making. Franz Dahlem, one of the Moscow team who had had responsibility for running the SED, was sacked. Rudolf Herrnstadt, editor of the party's newspaper, *Neues Deutschland*, and Wilhelm Zaisser, head of the State Security services, began agitating against Ulbricht.

Ulbricht fought back with a vengeance. In May, the SED party leadership, in the form of the 200 members of its Central Committee, came together in Berlin. They voted Ulbricht's way. Meeting amid reverberations from the crudely Stalinist show trials in Czechoslovakia, the Committee resolved to condemn what it called the destructive activities of persisting bourgeois elements, as well as Trotskyites, Zionists, and other 'traitors and morally depraved individuals'. It imposed an increase of at least 10 per cent on work norms and output, and it called for special celebrations to mark the sixtieth birthday of Walter Ulbricht.

But Ulbricht had overreached himself. Not only was his Politburo now split — despite the voting — but large swathes of the party membership were divided in their loyalties. Many of 'the workers' were disenchanted. Ulbricht's response was to publish a eulogy for Stalin in *Neues Deutschland*. The Soviet response to that was to propose that the GDR adopt an all-embracing package of social, political and economic reforms, a 'new course' which would offer a better deal to farmers and small business people, better relations with West Germany and, a critical point, with the church. It would also urge the refugees to return and try again.

But it was the increase in work norms which concerned the workers. Theirs was still a hard life and on their reading, the bourgeois elements were being promised new concessions, while there was no suggestion that the new norms should be revised. Sullenness turned to bitterness and bitterness to anger, and on 16 June 1953, at a building site on the Stalin-Allee, near the centre of East Berlin, the anger boiled over.

The Berlin uprising, as history has come to call it, is something I have discussed many times with East German friends. Their opinions vary. Thirty-five years on from the event itself, I reported some of their views in *The Guardian*. A pensioner friend said: 'I don't know why you harp on about it. It is not the problem now, because when it happened, we had no political foundation. People did not understand what the leadership expected of them.'

A university lecturer ten or more years younger than she was, laughed when he recalled that he and three others were expected to 'defend' a city centre office from attack by the mob, sacking and looting being widespread. 'The uprising', he told me, 'was the first crisis for post-war Socialism. For the people it is now too far away to matter; for the leadership, it remains vitally important as an experience and a lesson.'

I asked him, a party man, whether he thought such a thing could happen again. 'The extremes are not there,' he answered, 'and the tendency to strike has been outgrown. Our socio-economic development is basically good.'

The event itself was an exhilarating affair, marked by good humour, spontaneity and togetherness, until the Soviet tanks came in. Priests and policemen were among the participants as well as sceptics and party members. There was even a sprinkling of disenchanted Soviet troops.

The initial crowd was little more than 200 strong, and it came from one of the blocks on the Stalin-Allee building site. It was one of the city's most prestigious undertakings — 'the first socialist street' in Germany — but on the morning of 16 June the disgruntled group set off for the government quarter to demand a rescinding of the new work norms. Hundreds, and then thousands, of others joined them along the route, and soon there were shouts for free elections, for the sacking of the government, and, in some cases, for the blood of Walter Ulbricht.

Nightfall brought no change of mood and the following day there was a general strike call. Despite a prolonged cloudburst over the city centre, a number of leaderless and disorganised mass marches converged. Policemen, it is now said, threw their caps and their weapons into the River Spree and joined in. The Soviet flag was torn down from the top of the Brandenburg Gate and ceremonially burned. Until shortly before the tanks rolled in Unter den Linden and the Friedrichstrasse, even the Russians seemed to be enjoying themselves.

The mood changed abruptly when the first shots were fired. Anger which had been directed at the East German leadership was suddenly focused on the Soviet Army. Stones and lumps of masonry were thrown, and some demonstrators were run over by the tanks. The uprising began to fail because it had no recognisable leader around whom the people could rally. With a Soviet declaration of martial law, order was painfully restored.

The anger and frustration expressed in East Berlin — not without encouragement from the West — was repeated, with similarly violent results, in 270 towns and cities throughout the country. An unknown number, possibly several hundred, died. The gap between the workers and the party grew disconcertingly wider. Young people, who had formed a significant component part of the demonstration, were alienated.

It had blown up in a country which was still less than four years old. At its birth, Stalin had declared it to be 'the foundation stone for a united, democratic and peace-loving Germany'. Now, because Ulbricht did not have control of the appropriate forces, Soviet power was its suppressor. Amid the ensuing recriminations, it was the embryo People's Army, the State Security apparatus and the police who found the excuse they needed to demand more autonomy and growth, and their cause which was advanced.

While the uprising lasted, and while the dust swirled in its wake, Ulbricht kept his head down. Food prices were cut, reparations and national debts were cancelled – at the behest of the Russians. Then, while the West continued to rage against Soviet brutality, Ulbricht sought to strengthen his own hand. Once again, there were Party purges at every level, resulting in the dismissal of hundreds of thousands of members.

At this juncture, the Soviet leadership announced that it formally 'recognised' the sovereignty of the GDR. The new country, said an official decree from Moscow, would have the freedom, on its own initiative, to plan its internal developments and its external relations – including relations with West Germany. This led to the end of calls for German unity – from the East anyway – and the GDR joined the newly formed Warsaw Pact.

Control over 'internal developments' meant control over the economy. Since the Marshall Aid, extended under the European recovery programme, did not include East Germany, the Ulbricht leadership determined on a route which would turn the country into a valued producer of goods for its most dependable customer, the Soviet Union. Apart from poor-quality coal, and some uranium, there were precious few indigenous resources, and the decision was made to develop the potential of science and technology. The decision remains in force today: the enthusiasm for micro-electronics and computerisation is almost obsessional.

Late in 1955, nine months after the Russians had formally

announced that the 'state of war' between themselves and the Germans was at an end, Chancellor Adenauer took an ice-breaking West German delegation to Moscow. It led to the establishment of diplomatic relations between the Soviet Union and the Federal Republic and caused a quiver of concern in East Berlin. Just one week later, a GDR team was in Moscow, and the dismantling of the Soviet High Commission in East Berlin (which had succeeded the SMAD) was announced. The East German 'contribution' to keeping Soviet Army troops on their soil was cut by half.

The year 1957, when Khrushchev fought off a crisis of confidence in his own leadership in Moscow, saw further advances in East Germany. A number of new patterns for living and organisations were established. A forty-five-hour week was instituted, as were new relations between the centre, in East Berlin, and the provincial periphery. An economic council was formed to smooth out economic planning and management methods. The Free German Youth (the FDJ), which drills young people in the Communist way of thinking and doing things, was started. New controls were announced on the movement of *Grenzgänger*, people whose daily needs — whether a job, or a hair-do or a visit to the theatre — took them across the frontier which separated, more or less, the two Germanies.

In the following few years, and in various guises, the search was launched for a German 'peace treaty'. Khrushchev entered this particular fray with characteristic élan. He declared that Allied troops should leave West Berlin; he demanded separate peace treaties with each German state; and he supported calls from the Ulbricht administration for a non-aggression treaty between the two Germanies. These demands and gestures got nowhere and East-West truculence increased. Adenauer and Ulbricht led the skirmishes from the front.

In the spring of 1961, the Soviet leadership brought in new measures to restore their standing amongst the people of East Germany. They agreed to re-equip the GDR People's Army, to expand economic relations at bi-lateral level and to advance credits which would boost the still battered economy. The concern, clearly, was to strengthen the GDR, for the difficult and dangerous crisis which was to come. The German question, as Khrushchev told the US President, John Kennedy, that summer, was an 'ulcer' which had to be excised from 'the most dangerous spot in the world'.

Refugees were a class of people that Germans had grown wearily used to over the preceding sixteen years. Those who crossed from East Germany to West did so for a variety of reasons, none of which can have given much comfort to the Ulbricht leadership. It was a mass movement which was simultaneously discrediting him and, at least as important, was draining the lifeblood, and some of the best and youngest workers, from his economy. It has been calculated that more than 2.6 million people, very probably many more, left East Germany for the West between the founding of the GDR and the summer of 1961. Some went in search of a better job, some to rejoin members of their immediate family. Some went for political or religious reasons, seeking an end to the discrimination which had ruled their lives in the East.

As this movement gathered pace, Ulbricht conceded (in July) to his Central Committee that it had not yet proved possible to explain 'basic questions' of policy to the masses in such a way as to convince them. Apparently not — thousands were leaving the country every day. A month later he sought, and won, approval from the Communist Party leaders of every country in the Warsaw Pact for 'measures' to solve the West Berlin question.

On the night of 12-13 August 1961, the first reels of barbed wire were unrolled across Berlin's Potsdamer Platz (which had once been its Piccadilly Circus) and the carefully prepared military operation which led to the erection of the Berlin Wall had begun. West Berlin and West Germany were thus closed to the people of East Germany and while speeches of protest were made in the West, punctuated by tears of anguish on both sides, speeches were prepared in the East on how peace in Europe had been 'saved' by this extraordinary measure.

The Americans moved tanks right up to the new frontier but the statesmen of the West barely moved at all. Many were on holiday. Walter Ulbricht kept his head down, as he had done in 1953. He was now literally immured with one of the unhappiest populations in Europe. But he had real frontiers for the first time and the scope, if not the popularity, to map out a more secure future for the country he so controversially led.

Fourth Excursion: Meetings in Potsdam

I went to Potsdam on a clear, bright day and was unexpectedly reminded of Venice. This was not because of all the water in the vicinity, nor because of its faded glory, but because it is an airy place unlike anywhere else in Germany, and the yellows, ochres and muted shades of red with which its more imposing buildings have been surfaced, are refreshingly wholesome. It does not feel like a political city, or the place where, as some suggest, the Cold War started.

When the Prussians came in the early eighteenth century, it became a centre where the aristocracy would go to relax. But it also grew into a garrison town and spawned its own bureaucracy. Before that it had been little more than an extended fishing village. The locals made what living they could out of the waters of the Havel River which, in the Potsdam area, turned into great expanses of lake.

The Prussians, and Frederick the Great in particular, gave Potsdam palaces, parks and wide thoroughfares. In 1805 Napoleon's troops were here and helped themselves to some of its most precious *objets d'art*, a number of which were the work of a preceding group of Frenchmen, the Huguenots. In the Second World War, Allied bombs and Soviet shells inflicted untold damage on many of Potsdam's treasures, but much of the damage has been repaired. The tourists are back. It is now described by official East Germans as 'a socialist city of work, science, education and the arts'.

But as well as being a city of some style and elegance, it is also a place of perverse eccentricity. There are triumphal arches in the Roman style, bourgeois houses modelled on London's Whitehall, a water-works which looks more like a mosque, a tea-house in the 'Chinese' style, and houses in the Dutch quarter which must have made the settlers feel they had never left Holland.

Adolf Hitler staged one of his earliest, most theatrical 'events' in Potsdam. A few days before the passing of the Enabling Bill, which gave him full powers as Chancellor, he came to the Garrison Church here to consolidate his newly-won position in the grand manner. He sought, no doubt, a continuity in German history: Frederick the Great was buried here and Chancellor Bismarck opened the first Reichstag (or Parliament) here of the Second Reich of Wilhelm I.

The Führer-to-be chose a fine spring day. The city looked at its best, and there were swastika flags alternating with the black, white and red banners of the Kaisers. The aged President von Hindenburg attended and gave his blessing to the ceremony. An empty seat was kept for Wilhelm II, though he was not expected to appear. His son, the notional Crown Prince Wilhelm, on the other hand, played a full part in the proceedings, and stood alongside the President and the Chancellor to take the salute as the army marched past.

Today the square where this parade took place is quiet. There are flower gardens and fountains, and the war's damage to the church, a square red-brick affair, surmounted by a cathedral-like dome on columns, has been skilfully patched up. Tourist coaches are parked at one end. Some have come from West Berlin for an exorbitant price, but most have come from East Berlin. For Berliners, Potsdam is another jewel which they like to look at, and cherish, from time to time.

If you wander round it and look behind the façades, you become aware of the city's hidden ironies and occasional piquancy. It is not only that invading Frenchmen in the early 1800s took away artefacts made by their own Huguenot ancestors, or that the Dutch and the Russians (there is a beautiful Orthodox church), having contributed so much to the city's creation, became enemies during the course of World War Two. It is also the fact that European civilisation, of which Potsdam is a manifestation, is composed of separate pieces which, at human level, may seem incompatible. Potsdam is no exception.

Consider, for instance, the New Palace. It was built on the orders of Frederick in the 1760s as a sort of crowning point for the Sans Souci Park. It was an ostentatious gesture by him to the rest of Europe, a statement to the effect that even after a long and hard war, he still had enormous reserves. That war had been in Silesia which was invaded by Hitler once again in 1939, precipitating the Second World War.

When I last went, the palace — the essence of Prussian absolutism, according to GDR thinking — was covered in scaffolding. This time it was not because of past bombs or shells, but simply because time — and pollution — had caught up with the fabric and it was in need of attention. The irony on this occasion is that the attention is being given by a posse of guest workers — from Poland.

Sans Souci Park, in which this palace and other precious buildings are situated, was according to some accounts deliberately left out of the battle zone in the final siege of Berlin. In this way, the Soviet High Command prevented its destruction and also showed themselves to be guardians of cultural values. To such an extent, the legacy of the Hohenzollerns who still populate odd corners of the globe has been acknowledged. But these buildings will never be theirs again.

At the far end of the park, there is the Cecilienhof. To my mind, this mixture of private house and royal palace is one of Potsdam's most bizarre experiences, bringing together flair, perversity, and the vagaries of twentieth-century history under one roof. It is the one building in Europe where, in the space of less than thirty years, the late Kaiser and his family, high-ranking Nazis, and Josef Stalin with entourage, have all sought to make themselves at home. It has none of the lavishness of the palaces nearby and none of the exotica on its walls or shelves, but it is, as I see it, filled with the latency and the heaviness of the events that took place within its walls.

I was taken there in some style, in a chauffeur-driven Soviet limousine provided by the East German Travel Bureau at the end of 1988. It was a clear frosty morning and as we swept through the wooded parkland to the grand front door, I savoured the commanding view of one of the lakes. The Hohenzollerns also have their reasons to be wistful.

The building is modestly proportioned, made mainly of honey-coloured stone and Tudor-style timberwork on the upper storey. Ivy creeps up the walls and the windows are leaded. Bushes in the neat garden have been trimmed in the shape of birds and animals. There is a pervasive feeling of accessibility, almost domesticity, which may be familiar to those who know National Trust properties in Surrey or Sussex. However, instead of a latter-day Rudyard Kipling coming forward to greet me, it was a dapper little man in a dark grey lounge suit, his SED party badge gleaming on his lapel.

And here is another irony: Cecilienhof was erected during the very years that British and German armies were pounding hell out of each other during the First World War. It was begun in 1914, the time of naïve euphoria when the Kaiser and many Germans thought the engagement on the Western Front would be a short and sweet affair. It was completed as British troops pushed through against crumbling German resistance for the final and successful assault on the battered town of Ypres. This building was not intended to be a great royal palace; it was conceived, designed and constructed to be an English country house.

The architect was one Paul Schulze-Naumburg who spent some years in England before starting on the job. Later he was to make a great impression as a propagandist for the Nazi Party. The customer who wanted a Cecilienhof was Wilhelm II who, despite bombastic claims to be the ultimate arbiter in matters of 'taste', appears to have had no taste at all. He was, after all, Queen Victoria's eldest grandchild, was a frequent visitor to England, and he wanted an 'English' house which he could give as a present to his son, the Crown Prince Wilhelm, and his wife, Cecilie.

For little Willi, who liked to wear extrovert tweeds and plus-fours when duty allowed, the house was tailor-made. During the chaotic Weimar years, while his father pined away in exile at Doorn in the Netherlands, the younger couple made it their home. Even before Hitler came to power, Willi had sided with the Nazis and encouraged Wehrmacht generals and ranking members of the party and their families to come and stay. The house remained Hohenzollern property until 1945 and, it seems, residual members of the family still like to come and linger.

It was at this same Cecilienhof that the 1945 'Potsdam Conference' to formulate the occupation of the defeated Third Reich took place. This was only a matter of weeks after Berlin was finally taken, when Stalin made one of his rare excursions away from the Soviet Union. He was the main host, in the very heart of the Soviet-occupied area of the Third Reich, to America's President Truman and Britain's Winston Churchill, later to be replaced — after defeat in the General Election of July 1945 — by Clement Attlee. The Soviet leader, it is said, arrived in Tsar Nicholas's imperial train. There were Soviet soldiers and security men everywhere, for Stalin at this time was convinced that Hitler was still alive.

In the short time available, there had been no time to remove much of the furniture and fittings, though extra needs were met by taking furniture from other Potsdam palaces. Hundreds of the Hohenzollerns' collection of books, many of them in English and dating from the 1920s and 1930s, are still there today. The windows, which were stripped of their lead lattice-work by the Soviet security men who wanted a better view of what was going on, are today re-leaded. The furniture in the conference area remains much as it was. Upstairs, Cecilie's amazing tiled bathroom, with steps down to her gold-tapped bath, is still as she last used it.

Attlee, when he arrived, described the house as 'stock exchange gothic', and would be amused to know that two-thirds of the whole complex is now one of East Germany's most exclusive hotels — it was the manager who greeted me at the door — while the remainder is kept as a memorial to the conference.

The victorious warriors came together in the main hall of the house, high-ceilinged, wood-panelled and sombre in atmosphere. It is dominated still by the large circular table round which the talking went on. Nobody, it has since been noted, said anything publicly during the conference about dividing Germany into two. But nothing seemed to happen to prevent the division from taking place. Churchill was the most talkative delegate and Stalin the most reticent. Truman was much preoccupied with the likely impact of the atomic bomb which had just been satisfactorily tested in New Mexico.

In the evenings, the conference delegates demonstrated that

they were also human beings. Dinners were given at which the host of the evening was clearly determined to outshine the other two. Truman brought in a pianist and a violinist to serenade his guests. Stalin, when his turn came, brought in two pianists and two violinists. Churchill brought an entire band of the Royal Air Force. Stalin was not amused.

The delegations' respective quarters in the Cecilienhof are open to view. Stalin's group was based in the imperial writing room. It is now decorated in shades of Soviet red and the huge desk which dominates it is the one which Stalin used. A map of uncertain date hangs on the wall, showing a Germany divided into four occupation zones. The room in 1988 seemed distinctly shabby, the floor unswept, and a button was missing from the upholstery of the settee.

The Americans were allocated a main sitting room and adjoining smoking room. It is predominantly a rather harsh green in decoration, and this fact, together with the relative sparseness of the furnishings, makes it feel cooler than the Soviet area, but it is better kept. Further permutations on how a defeated Germany might be carved up still hang on the wall.

Churchill and company had the former library and reading room. His ornate and delicately made desk has an unexpectedly ecclesiastical air about it, and the matching chair, my guide said to me with a giggle, was too narrow to be of much use to Churchill himself. The British Prime Minister's first act on entering, we are told, was to flop into an armchair on the balcony and ask for a whisky.

Certainly the quarters seem to be the most 'homely' of the three. There is a stag at bay in the fireplace, and the books, if he had had the time, would have titillated Churchill's catholic tastes. *Sailing, Service Life in Malta,* and *Retreat from Glory* were three titles I noted at random: the last of them conveyed something that was somehow, in this context, tantalisingly symbolic.

In GDR political thinking, the memorial is a hallowed place. Mikhail Gorbachev, on his first full visit to the country as Soviet Communist Party leader in 1986, made a point of calling at the Cecilienhof and, as he stood with his wife, Raisa, nicely framed in the English doorway, of catching the eye of the world's television cameramen. The rhododendrons behind him were just beginning to flower.

East German polemicists routinely use the place to make significant political points. It is a well-known fact, they say, that 'reactionary forces' in the US, Britain and France violated the Potsdam Agreement, and it is another well-known fact that the Agreement has been fulfilled in the Soviet Occupation Zone, the present GDR. A third fact, not much touched upon but ineluctably true, is that it is Stalin's face which dominates the exhibition area and his presence that seems to lurk most strongly. It is strange, still, that he seemed to have least to say.

It is a relief to leave the faintly claustrophobic atmosphere of the memorial and re-enter the hotel. Here, the dark oak beams, the grand staircase and the carpeting, though sanitised in the peculiarly East German way, are more reassuring, almost homely. The hotel manager invited me to join him for lunch and we perused, with ritual amusement, a menu which offered Russian, British and American alternatives — respectively, fish soup and pork (for 30 East marks), curried bird's nest soup and turkey (29 marks) and ham and tournedos (32 marks). The Russian dish, he insisted, was the most popular.

The manager showed me family photographs of the Hohenzollern family and said that when the house was opened, in 1917, the family was on its last imperial legs. 'There was no bally-hoo at the opening,' he said, 'because the people of Potsdam were living a very poor life at that time. They had nothing to eat except sugar beet.' Then he produced a well-thumbed back number of the English gentry's magazine, *Country Life.* 'Your country houses often become hotels,' mused the manager. 'The same thing happens here!'

As we ate, we discussed bits and pieces of German, British, and Soviet political history. Potsdam, I learned, was Karl Liebknecht's constituency when he was a Reichstag deputy. After the Second World War, it became the black market capital of Europe. The Queen of England is still regularly honoured with dinners thrown by British officers at the Cecilienhof on her birthday. Gorbachev, he said, was 'probably the best news to hit the Communist movement since Marx and Engels'.

And, having told me these things, the manager asked me a favour. Would I, on my return home, please send him a recipe for Yorkshire pudding? It was something extra he would like to be able to offer on the Cecilienhof menu.

Beyond the Wall

Walter Ulbricht claimed, some months after August 1961, that he had no alternative but to build the Wall. But he also claimed that its installation had brought him the deepest humiliation of his career, that every bullet fired at a would-be escaper was a bullet in his own foot. Nikita Khrushchev, who had his own differences with Ulbricht but who in this exercise had been a close collaborator, acknowledged that the Wall was perhaps 'a defect' and that it was ugly to the beholder.

The first version was barbed wire and precariously balanced breeze-blocks, but it was enough to give the East German authorities, and the Russians, the physical security they both required. The leadership in East Berlin, and especially the economic planners, knew they at last had a predictable workforce and that foundations could be laid for a more positive economic future. The leadership in Moscow, in contemplating any threat from the West, knew that the further outposts of the Warsaw Pact were that much stronger and more impenetrable than they had been before.

None of these considerations diminished the anguish and deep unhappiness felt by millions of ordinary East Germans. There were tears in many homes. But once again there were carefully prepared meetings in factories, offices and farms to explain what had been done. For the Communists who had most of the explaining to do, the task was immense. In human terms, hundreds of thousands of Germans had been summarily cut off from their nearest and dearest; in ideological terms, a decree devised and ordered by a nebulous group of functionaries above and out of reach of the people had been carried out with ruthless efficiency. The people did not respond by taking to the streets, as they had in 1919 and 1953, but by turning in upon themselves. The gulf that had been created between the rulers and the ruled as a result of 1953 grew still wider in the autumn of 1961.

It was not to be very long before old-age pensioners, a group of little economic importance, were allowed to make short visits to the West, but it was soon clear there was no way in which the Wall could be explained in strictly Marxist-Leninist terms. Even if some of the rationalisations given did eventually take on a certain plausibility, and even if many East Germans did in time get used to its existence, the Communist movement, in human terms, has never quite got over the shock.

One of the biggest political ironies of the year in which the Wall was built lies in the fact that it was also the year in which de-Stalinisation moved into gear. Perhaps Stalin himself would have approved of the Wall, but the eradication of the cult of his own personality, which advanced a long way in precisely the same period, was something else.

For Khrushchev, the removal of Stalin's body from the mausoleum he had shared with Lenin in Moscow's Red Square was the culmination of a process he had initiated with his so-called 'secret speech' five years before. For the East German leadership, whose thinking owed so much to Stalin, that process continued on a wet November night when all visible traces of the former Soviet leader were removed from East Germany. The Stalin-Allee in Berlin could not be dismantled, of course, but the huge bronze statue of Stalin which had dominated it was pulled down, broken into pieces and carted away into oblivion. Stalinstadt, where a Soviet-built steel mill smelts Soviet ore, was renamed Eisenhütten-stadt. A few lines in *Neues Deutschland* were considered enough to signal such a fundamental change.

Perhaps it was de-Stalinisation in the air, perhaps it was the new political elbow room that was now at their disposal — no one can be sure — but the East German leadership opted for yet another 'new course'. The aim was 'the complete and comprehensive building of socialism' and, in the glowing words of the new party programme, published in 1962, it would have a human face. 'Socialism,' the programme announced, 'is the result of countless good deeds by millions of people. It is the conscious and planned realisation of all ideals of freedom and the progressive efforts of the German people. It is the transition into the realm of true humanity, equality and fraternity, of peace and freedom.'

Ulbricht's mentors in the Soviet Union were meanwhile entertaining their own ideas of reform. In late 1962, nearly a quarter of a century before the advent of Gorbachev's perestroika, something closely resembling it was being floated in the columns of *Pravda* by an economist teaching at the University of Kharkov, Evsei Liberman. In a radical departure from orthodox thinking, he advocated that consideration should be given to more autonomy for production unit managers, with more control over their own resources — in money, men and materials — and more say in what was produced. Customer requirements, he indicated, rather than planners' norms should get priority.

Many East Europeans — except perhaps the Poles — like to depict their economies as being far more manoeuvrable than that of the giant Soviet Union. It is the difference, they say, between a rowing boat and an ocean-going liner. Perhaps this was a concept which appealed to East Germany's helmsmen; certainly, it remained in favour, with occasional modifications, throughout the 1960s.

The total restructuring of the national economy which was now required led to the principles of a 'New Economic System' of planning and management being adopted. It led to special emphasis being placed on export-orientated producers, and by 1964, East Germany was being hailed by the Russians as 'one of the strongest industrial states in Europe'. The enthusiasts for the new ideas tended to be the educated younger generation. The older generation were motivated by pristine ideological considerations and were more wary and conservative. A new 'event', in other words, was dividing East German society, separating more rigid elements from those who wanted reform.

Intermittently, the rowing boat found itself on choppy waters, and political developments, at home and abroad, did not help the reformists keep course. The conservatism of the older generation, even at this relatively early stage in the country's life, was only one factor. Another was the abrupt departure of Khrushchev from the

Kremlin in October 1964. His going meant that the anti-reformist, heavy-industry ministers in the Soviet Union — and the GDR — could fight their corner with renewed vigour. There was too a fear in East Berlin that the sort of reform virus that was soon to grip Hungary and, albeit briefly, Czechoslovakia, might have a negative effect in East Germany. Ulbricht was to be one of the fiercest opponents of Alexander Dubcek and the Prague Spring.

By 1970, ministers were forced to admit that the country's managers were not performing as the system expected. The ministers were led by Willi Stoph, a former bricklayer and old-school Communist who had taken over as Prime Minister when Otto Grotewohl, the old SPD leader, died in 1964. Stoph repeated his views at a meeting of the party leadership and was obliged to watch as the central planners took back some of the powers they had surrendered some years before. By the end of the year, the 'New Economic System', patched up and modified as it was, had to be abandoned.

Politically, the 1960s was to be a period of stabilisation in East Germany. The decade had not begun well. The recovery from the enforced building of the Wall was never total. You can see the evidence for this is in the eyes of the people who come in the evenings to the East Berlin side of the Brandenburg Gate to watch the sun setting over the inaccessible West. But approaching acceptance has been achieved. It is, I have been told, like learning to live with an amputation.

Cursory soundings at grassroots level at this time would show that ideals belonged to the past, probably lost for ever in the hard times of the 1930s and the 1940s. There was ample cause for disenchantment, but there were still men and women coming forward, often for very private reasons, to join the ruling party. Membership at this time showed a steady increase.

Occasional voices were raised to echo those which had been heard in the party leadership of the pre-Nazi period, rejecting too much Soviet interference in German affairs. For some, a Khrushchev rebuff to Ulbricht in mid-1964 had somehow been satisfying even if it was only minimal. The East German leader had wanted a peace treaty with the Soviet Union, but the Soviet leader, who could be just as persistent in the pursuit of a desired objective, would go only as far as a treaty of friendship and co-operation. Ulbricht made do with that, but in four months Khrushchev was gone.

The takeover by the colourless Leonid Brezhnev signalled the beginning of what are now called the Soviet Union's 'years of stagnation', 1964–1982. From the foreign policy point of view, these years were not initially all that stagnant, for there was an identifiable Soviet response to the Ostpolitik of West Germany's Willy Brandt, which he conducted first as Foreign Minister and latterly as an SPD Chancellor. Brezhnev liked to say he was leading a 'peace offensive'.

There was undiluted anger in East Berlin at the beginning of 1967 when the West Germans and the Romanians decided to establish diplomatic relations. Within a matter of months, the East Germans had secured new friendship treaties with Czechoslovakia, Poland, Hungary and Bulgaria. These developments, too, cemented the division of Germany and underlined the divisions of Europe.

The heady 'Spring', and then the invasion crisis, in Czechoslovakia in 1968 — in which the West Germans were also heavily implicated — was deeply problematical for the East German leadership. At grassroots level, there was as much interest in and sympathy for what Alexander Dubcek was trying to do in Czechoslovakia as there was in most European countries. Ulbricht himself was trying on reformist clothes but they fitted nothing like as convincingly as those which had adorned Dubcek in Prague. The stiff old Saxon was no match for the lean and supple Slovak.

On his seventy-fifth birthday, long eulogies to Ulbricht were published in the East German press and his praises were sung by distinguished people from all walks of life — from artists and painters to scientists and factory managers. Fellow members of the politburo, who were not exempt, must have felt a sense of *déjà vu*.

The Czechoslovak developments were worrying to Ulbricht partly because an important precursor to them had been the removal of Antonin Novotny from the Communist Party leadership in Prague. He was a contemporary of Ulbricht with a similar background and values. There was more worry because it was Novotny's dismissal that had indirectly paved the way for Dubcek's so-called 'Action Programme'. This advocated freedom from censorship, freedom to travel, more economic reform and the formal rehabilitation of the 'victims' of Stalin. Though East Germany at this time had probably the highest standard of living in the whole Comecon area, there were elements in the Czechoslovak programme which would have provoked chaos in the country and Ulbricht was quick to endorse — if he did not initiate — Warsaw Pact criticisms of the new Prague line.

The August invasion was a matter of consternation to Communists worldwide. East Europeans, some in responsible official positions, were ashamed that their country's army should have participated and many handed in their party membership cards. The East German party had not been contaminated by the Prague virus, but a new generation (since 1953) now had reason for disenchantment.

Not, however, in every case. Some years after the event, I asked one East German friend what had been his reaction when the invasion took place. 'Easy,' he replied. 'I joined the SED. I knew then that everything it stood for was at low ebb and they welcomed me with open arms. I would be well-placed to seek change from inside rather than outside.' (This friend was later delighted by the arrival in power of Gorbachev, though puzzled by the lukewarm welcome from his fellow countrymen.)

While the West wrung its hands for Czechoslovakia, the countries of the Warsaw Pact — including, most vociferously, East Germany — accelerated the pace of international discussion on questions relating to European security. It was a satisfying platform for the East Germans to speak from, because it would be a legitimate means of canvassing for wider diplomatic recognition.

The problem now was the energy of Willy Brandt. Suddenly West Germans and East Germans seemed to be arguing, or rather sparring, on equal terms. On humane grounds alone, German calling to German could not be ignored. Willi Stoph, who was still Ulbricht's Prime Minister, went so far as to suggest that Brandt was in fact adopting a 'realistic' approach and should be heard. Ulbricht did not agree and it took a Soviet intervention to facilitate the meeting between Brandt and Stoph which finally took place, in March 1970, in Erfurt.

That meeting taught the East German leadership a great deal

about the country it ran. The biggest crowds by far that the security forces had yet had to contend with filled the streets and squares of Erfurt. The people's enthusiasm to see and to acclaim 'Willy' was almost overwhelming. It was to be a talking point for those who were there for many years to come.

The crowds when Stoph came to Kassel in West Germany were nothing like as numerous, enthusiastic or single-minded as they had been in Erfurt. Stoph did not have the charisma of Brandt, which he could not help. But nor did the regime which he represented excite people's curiosity. West Germans felt they knew enough about East Germany, and besides, a sizeable number had already turned their back on it and walked away. For thinking East Germans it was a salutary experience.

Less than a year after the second Brandt-Stoph meeting, which marked the beginning of a new relationship between the two Germanies, Walter Ulbricht was finally forced to step down. From the Kremlin, he had come to be regarded as the tiresome general on the front line. Reports coming back from the Soviet Ambassador in East Berlin, Pyotr Abrasimov, painted Ulbricht in disagreeable colours. His ambitions for his country were undeniable, but they were paramount and they did not always coincide with Soviet ambitions in the area of détente and East-West relations generally.

At the end of his career, he was autocratic and strangely alone. He was also an anachronism, having entered political life before the First World War, and then studied in Moscow when Lenin was still alive. In power he had survived, and prospered, under Stalin, had argued and won against the volatile Khrushchev, and was unscathed under Brezhnev. If that implied flexibility, then Ulbricht was flexible.

But economically as well as politically there were 'shortcomings' in the GDR performance in the late Ulbricht years. Output in the crucial infrastructural areas of energy, iron and steel and construction was below planned targets. This had a knock-on effect in dependent industries and gave rise to what officials call 'negative socio-political consequences', which was a way of saying that there were nasty confrontations with political overtones on the factory floor — and this at a time when there were workers rioting in the Polish shipyards. In addition, trade obligations to the Soviet Union were not being met. This led to further strains on the bi-lateral relationship.

Erich Honecker took over at the beginning of May 1971, a man unlike Ulbricht in almost every way, though he had won his trust and joined his politburo as a full member more than a dozen years before. A youthful fifty-eight on taking office, he was the son of a Saarland coalminer and he had been a committed and active Communist — according to his official biography — since the age of ten. Before he was twenty he had already spent nearly a year in Moscow, returning to Berlin just before the Nazis came to power to run the party's youth organisation. In the mid-1930s, however, the Nazis tracked him down and imprisoned him. He spent the Second World War in a Brandenburg jail.

After the war he was one of the local Communists picked upon to do responsible work, resuming once again his activities with the party youth. He joined the Central Committee of the SED in the first year of its existence and was a candidate member of the politburo four years later. To that extent, he owes his position, if not to Stalin himself, then certainly to Stalinist patronage.

His career has not been that of a headstrong reformist. He is no intellectual, and in many ways he has remained a consistent and staunchly pro-Soviet conservative. By inclination he keeps his powder dry, though he is less colourless than he used to be. In the early 1970s he did not like being photographed. By the 1980s, I saw for myself how he obviously enjoys the attentions, and the company, of press photographers.

By the time Mikhail Gorbachev took over in Moscow, Honecker had already proved himself as a survivor. He had advanced while others suffered or faltered during the early purges of the party, and the 1953 uprising, in which large numbers of his FDJ youth organisation were visibly involved and which could therefore have jeopardised his career, was merely a little local difficulty along the way. The de-Stalinisation campaign which began in earnest in 1956 may have disconcerted him — but not for long. In 1958, when he gained full politburo membership, he was given responsibility for security services and the armed forces. In that capacity he was prime organiser of the building of the Berlin Wall.

One of Ulbricht's main struggles had been to have East Germany accepted as the GDR by a wider world. Honecker's concern, almost from the outset, has been to have the GDR better accepted by its own inhabitants. He has done this by appealing to their innate sense of discipline (one of his favourite words) and control. Even since the mid-1960s, his public pronouncements have emphasised the need, as he had seen it, to foster the specifically GDR identity, to go it alone with a sense of pride and without looking over one's shoulder to see how the West Germans are doing.

There were significant straws in the wind in the summer before he came to power. In July 1970 it was announced that exported goods would no longer be labelled 'Made in Germany', but 'Made in the GDR'. Six months after his takeover, Station Germany began broadcasting as Voice of the GDR; German Television became GDR Television, and the German Culture Association became the GDR Culture Association. Then, after the signing of the four-power agreement on Berlin in 1972, it was decided that West Germans would have to have visas, rather than daily passes, to visit East Berlin.

The GDR, in other words, was beginning to take control of its own destiny. The four-power agreement found it secure enough to open its doors wider to visitors from West Berlin for humanitarian and family reasons, as well as tourism. Postal and travel arrangements between the two Germanies were made less complicated, and it was announced that the millions of East Germans who had left their country 'illegally' before 1972 would no longer be prosecuted if they reappeared to visit relatives or friends.

At the end of 1972, the basic Treaty between the two German States was signed. This meant that the GDR and the Federal Republic, as now formally agreed, would henceforth respect each other's independence and would develop 'normal' relations on the basis of equality. It also meant the GDR was officially recognised as having the separate existence it had proclaimed for itself back in 1949. There was understandable rejoicing in the streets, but there was no end, among many officials of my acquaintance anyway, of the continuing need to prove something.

Both states applied for membership of the United Nations —

something which was finally granted to the GDR and to the Federal Republic nine months later. Diplomatic recognition was being accorded by an increasing number of countries. In 1972, a total of twenty-three mainly Third World countries indicated that they would be exchanging ambassadors. In 1973, twice as many countries, including most West Europeans, made the same move. Britain was the sixty-ninth country to do so in February 1973, following Ethiopia and Malta and preceding France and Nigeria. The US did not make its move until September 1974, a full six months after the Federal Republic agreed to open its permanent representative's office in East Berlin.

(Despite this recognition, it is worth noting that by mid-1989, a US President has still not been to East Berlin, and neither has a British Prime Minister. Nor, for that matter, has the East German leader been to either Washington or London — though senior East German officials frequently made it plain in private conversations that such visits would be more than welcome as far as the GDR was concerned.)

At a more down to earth level Honecker, who is himself decidedly short in stature, began in the 1970s to take an interest in the 'little man'. In his own youth his trade had been that of a roof repairer. As leader he set about trying to re-establish a meaningful role in the ruling party for the working class it was intended to represent.

In his first three years after taking over, he effected several reshuffles at the top — accelerating the pace of change after the death of Ulbricht in 1973. Horst Sindermann, who shared Honecker's background (including also a ten-year spell in a Nazi prison), became Prime Minister, replacing the strong-minded Willi Stoph. In addition, several close associates of the new leader were elevated by him either in the government or in the party apparatus. In the mid-1970s, Honecker seemed to have an administration of men, and a few women, whom he knew and could trust.

The controversial status of Ulbricht persisted even after his death. This came in 1973 and it was an event which presented Germans and others with a chance to reflect on the nature of his mixed achievement, and it gave a glimpse into the standing of

Communism in Germany and Europe at that particular moment. Suddenly, no one seemed quite sure how great a man he was; for several weeks there was argument about what to do with his mortal remains.

In the end, he joined the late Wilhelm Pieck in the out-of-the-way Socialists' cemetery at Friedrichsfelde. Though it was a state funeral, it was a comparatively quiet affair: there were no ponderous eulogies as there had been for his seventy-fifth birthday, and there were no official mourners from other countries. In 1988, however, on the ninety-fifth anniversary of his birth, old grudges were put to one side, and a glowing tribute to 'the great son of the working class' filled half a page of *Neues Deutschland*.

There was a clear shift in the substance of public debate after Honecker's takeover — something which was not necessarily of his making, but which he did nothing to obstruct. The shift occurred partly as a result of the growing contacts with West Germany and partly because, as he himself acknowledged, East Germans with the flick of a switch any night of the week could see and digest West German television or radio in preference to the GDR product. East Germans are avid television watchers.

The repercussions of this technological penetration are many and varied. By the time Mikhail Gorbachev was preaching the virtues of glasnost and open debate in the mid-1980s, it was already an established fact of life in East Germany. 'Opposition' points of view or their equivalent can be heard in every home without any prosecution being brought. East Germans, in other words, are 'better informed' than their counterparts in, say, Czechoslovakia.

This has led to a situation where for many the wish to emigrate, which Western politicians have made so much of, has been blurred. For many others, that wish has undoubtedly been sharpened. I have had many conversations with young East Germans who say they are now more determined than ever to go and 'have a look' at the realities of West Germany. Unofficial estimates put the figure at well over a million.

The Ulbricht leadership may have rejected, with the then Soviet leadership and that of other Warsaw Pact members, the 'human face' of socialism as adumbrated in Czechoslovakia in 1968, but it still paid lip service and more to what it called the 'socialist human community' and 'the developed social system'. Honecker, with some politburo support, redrafted this formulation and chose from the very beginning of his tenure to influence 'social development' as profoundly as he could. His aim became clear by the mid 1980s: it was somehow to fuse economic and social progress into one.

Ulbricht thought the transition to Communism in East Germany might be manageably short, possibly helped along the way by the Liberman reforms which were being discussed in the Soviet Union. Honecker thought otherwise. His message was that 'material and cultural' levels could be improved through increased output, greater efficiency, more scientific and technological progress, and higher productivity. His aim was 'the developed socialist society', the establishment of which would be character-ised by 'far-reaching political, economic, social, intellectual and cultural changes'.

The 'leading role of the party', which is a sacrosanct area where ideologists tread only with great respect, has been given increased emphasis under Honecker. Many party members, and especially those in executive functions in a party unit, take their duties very seriously, even solemnly. The number who stick rigorously to the rules and work as closely as they should — according to these rules — with the state security apparatus is of course difficult to determine. In my own contacts I have always been wary, and sought to restrain myself, when in the company of those who sport the little badge and ask me penetrating questions and then proceed to glaze over as the conversation progresses. Those who genuinely enjoy a good argument are something else.

One of the party's problems under Honecker, exacerbated by the Western TV presence, is the growing political awareness of the average East German. This is illustrated not in the art of graffiti as it is in West Germany — the East side of the Wall, partly because it is largely inaccessible, is completely blank — but in acute aware-ness, for instance, of what Gorbachev is trying to achieve when he talks of democratisation. His works are much sought after at international book fairs. It is also shown by young people in their knowledge of, and ability to recite by heart, the political messages that are embedded in current rock music.

The question of reconciling the leading role of the party with the wish to involve more and more people in the decision-forming process is therefore very tricky. Kurt Hager, one of the politburo's septuagenarian ideologists, spoke in late 1983 of the socialist society as one which was continually and extensively developing, 'alive' and 'in a constant state of movement'. At the same time, however, the SED (a state within a state) has to keep control, and the Honecker faith in 'discipline' presumably remains inviolate.

By the mid-1980s, Honecker and others were claiming that there was intense Soviet interest in East German planning and management methods. There was less public allusion to the fact that the economy was slowing down, partly as a result of the world trade recession, that East Germany was running up substantial dollar debts to Western creditors, and that living standards, which Honecker promised to raise, were stagnating.

Constitutional changes in 1974 had meant that the GDR, aged twenty-five, would no longer be referred to as 'a socialist state of the German nation' but as 'a socialist state of peasants and workers'. And, having gone this far, Honecker went further. History, he decided, could also be refurbished. Not only was Martin Luther honoured on the 500th anniversary of his birth, but so was Beethoven on the 200th anniversary of his ('the GDR,' said the party newspaper, 'is Beethoven's true home' — even though he was born in the West German capital, Bonn). A full-length, widely acclaimed biography of the arch anti-Socialist, Bismarck, was also published in the GDR. At street level, the interest in history is insatiable.

Ten years later, this sense of self-satisfaction was taken a stage further: 'Socialism in the GDR,' announced an official party and government declaration to coincide with the thirty-fifth birthday of the country itself, 'is the heir and the continuer of all that is good, progressive, humane and democratic in history, because it does itself embody progress, democracy and humanity. The creative relationship with German history and with the world's history is an essential element of our Socialist national consciousness.'

Accept that, the declaration seemed to be saying, and you will be in no doubt about the 'legitimacy' of the GDR. This message was further reinforced when Mikhail Gorbachev came to East

Berlin for the 1986 Congress of the SED. He found the leadership in a mood of unabashed self-congratulation, declaring themselves the 'most successful' party on German soil, leading a country which was both 'politically stable' and 'economically efficient'.

Gorbachev, by his presence, affirmed Honecker's position. Honecker, by supervising the appointment of more of his known supporters to the policy-making politburo, underwrote that affirmation. There was a deferential good nature between the two men — so very different in background and yet each so convinced that he was on the 'right road' to Communism. Smiles came easily — in public anyway.

The year of that Congress saw the twenty-fifth anniversary of the erection of the Berlin Wall. Not unexpectedly, there were a number of Western statements, official and less official, to the effect that the Wall should be pulled down. Honecker was ready and, having called a meeting of army, police and frontier guards, declared that the 'measures' taken when the Wall was built were in the service of peace. They had facilitated a shift from confrontation to détente, he said, and they served European security.

Three years later, as the European security talks came to an end in Vienna, there were again calls for the Wall to come down. Once again, Honecker was ready. The Wall, he told the US and other critics in early 1989, would stay for as long as the reasons for its existence persisted — 'for another fifty if not 100 years'. Visiting West Germany some months later, Gorbachev also spoke about the Wall, and said he could imagine the day when the need for it would disappear. 'Nothing is eternal,' he said.

Honecker's truculence towards the West was balanced by a dash of assertiveness towards the East when the Russians marked the seventieth anniversary of the Great Revolution of 1917. The GDR, Honecker told Gorbachev, followed 'with great interest and sympathy' the Soviet Union's 'further advance on the road to socialism'. Was he saying, asked a mischievous friend in East Berlin, 'Keep up the good work and you'll soon be at our level'? No one was totally sure.

PART TWO

On German Soil

Among the People

East Germans are hard-working. The statistics prove it. They put in an average of between forty and forty-three hours a week, depending on the nature of their job, and the rest of their time, if party precepts are taken at all literally, is spent enjoying whatever is on offer 'for the good of the working class and the happiness of the people'.

This does not mean everybody is glowing and smiling all the time. Far from it. Jobs can be onerous, carried out with obsolete equipment or in less than ideal surroundings, and home life can be in a run-down tenement block where you have to wait to use the outside lavatory. But unemployment, according to Erich Honecker, is a concept from an 'alien' world and housing, as 'a social problem', should be solved by the end of 1990.

The daytime, it should be said, is the prime time for being sociable. Camaraderie on the shop floor and in offices is strong. In town centres supplies, even of rudimentary necessities, are not dependable, but there are always people milling about, their curiosity fuelled by shortages, anxious to see what is available.

In the early evening, especially in the winter, the air begins to be permeated with the acrid smell of brown coal. Question the smell and you will be told that the quality of the stuff was never particularly good and, anyway, the best of it has been mined. Universally used, it burns well, but it is smoky and the main cause of East Germany's major pollution problems.

In the course of the evening, the streets slowly empty of people. Live entertainment venues are invariably well patronised, eating and drinking places likewise. Otherwise the big draw is West German television.

How, apart from bald statistics, does one convey the quality of East German life? One way is to describe service in shops and catering establishments. Unlike the Soviet Union (where it is almost non-existent) or Poland (where it is offhand and uninterested), it is generally good and people care. The courtesy shown may seem peremptory; but it is courtesy nevertheless.

Another way is to look at the environment in which everyday life is supposed to function. You can't avoid the queues: mealtimes, even in East Berlin, are tiresome if you want more than a stand-up snack. You can wait as much as half an hour for a free table, before you can sit down, to wait for the waiter. Public transport leaves much to be desired, with the stampede to get a seat on a crowded train or bus leading to chaos as it meets the stampede to get off. But food in the cafés and restaurants is usually reassuringly good, and transport is extremely cheap.

In 1988 I wrote in my notebook about Leipzig (the country's second biggest city): 'Five- and six-storey blocks, black, pockmarked and visibly crumbling; should have been demolished or vigorously refurbished years ago. Are still homes for many. Flats are often well-furnished with inherited or custom-built pieces. Entrances grim, dirty and dark. Pavements are clean but broken and uneven, sometimes dangerous; pushing a pram looks like hard work. Road surfaces badly holed and worn, but navigable. In the wet countryside, mud, mud, mud.'

On the next page: 'Above a shop doorway, dark red Gothic lettering on a faded yellow glass background says: Adalbert Taubig, Tischlermeister. It is obviously decades since he practised his trade. Will he return?'

These are the facts: the country's population, on 1 January 1988, was 16,661,423, with women outnumbering men by 8.8 million to 7.9 million. It is a population which, with one or two exceptional years, has been gradually falling since the country came into being in 1949. Indeed, the total is still fractionally less than the number who lived on the same land area in 1939.

Between two and three million East Germans are calculated to have crossed from East to West — most of them before the Wall went up. An unknown number, but certainly running into tens of thousands altogether, have come the other way. Those going West, as the leadership has intermittently, and bitterly, acknowledged, have included a large proportion of young and skilled people. In addition, the Americans 'recruited' a number of very able scientists and technical personnel, as did the Russians.

Almost six million East Germans have been born since the 1961 Wall. Almost half the population have never known life without it. Slightly under ten per cent of the population were alive in the Kaiser's time. Many have Polish and Slav-sounding surnames, which suggests they were among the refugees who even in the last century had begun to arrive from Silesia or from the previously 'German' parts of Czechoslovakia. Still more of them arrived after 1945.

There are 6.5 million households, of which more than half consist of only one or two persons. Beyond these, the vast majority of families have only one or two children, rarely more. There are about 140,000 marriages a year — and slightly over 50,000 divorces. About one in four of all single men and women are co-habiting, something which the authorities see as 'more practical' than getting engaged. 'We are going to have to come to terms with the fact that many people are not going to keep one partner all their lives,' said Dr Jutta Gysi, an establishment sociologist in 1988. 'The number of second or third marriages, people living together and one-parent families is bound to increase. I see this phenomenon as an expression of very dynamic social progress.'

Today there is almost no poverty in the GDR, though some pensioners, especially those unable to obtain the perks and little comforts available through day trips to the West, find it hard to make ends meet. The average national income per head, cautiously based on official exchange rates, came to about $8130 in 1986, easily the highest in the Warsaw Pact area. The figure is $630 a head above Czechoslovakia, which is next highest, and more than twice the figure for Bulgaria or the Soviet Union.

Finding somewhere to live seems to be easier in East Germany than elsewhere in East Europe and, proportionately, East Germans have more television sets, washing machines and telephones at their disposal. However, certain shops — notably for food and clothing — are better stocked in Czechoslovakia and Hungary, for instance, and the waiting list for a car can be shorter than the

several years it takes in East Germany. About nine households out
of every twenty have a car.

In all these countries, however, the stated availability of
consumer goods needs to be treated with a pinch of salt. Even items
that are less than exotic may only be obtainable from the more
expensive luxury shops (now proliferating in the chic Nikolaiviertel of East Berlin) or in the hard-currency Intershops.

The black market in goods and services is not so obvious in East
Germany as it is elsewhere in Eastern Europe, and I strongly
suspect there is less bribery and corruption than, for instance,
in Poland. Nevertheless, it does seem possible — with persistence —
to obtain interesting food, clothing and consumer goods.

For those who do not have the right contacts, Honecker
declared in 1986 that 'customers' needs must be attended to more
promptly and satisfactorily'. But even as he spoke, I noted when I
reported this speech, there were queues waiting in the rain in the
Nikolaiviertel just two hundred yards away.

East Germans eat well. They eat more meat and vegetables than
their West German counterparts and drink more spirits. They
drink about the same amount of beer — about a litre every two
days for every man, woman and child in the country — and they
sing jolly German drinking songs at the drop of a hat. They take
much less tea and coffee than the West Germans.

Entertainment, when it is not time spent in front of the
television set or the dinner table, could well be in the cinema —
which the 'average' East German visits four times a year. But he, or
she, goes much more rarely to the theatre (in spite of Brecht going
on for ever), making only one visit every two years and only every
other one of these visits is to see something which is not opera or
operetta.

East Germans go to the zoo more often than they go to the
theatre, and to museums — statistically speaking — still more often.
But museums, it should be noted, are frequently the habitat of
large groups of small schoolchildren who, if they are not pulling
each other's hair, look bored to tears. Only one East German in
three frequents a library and the average household contains,
according to people who must be among the world's most zealous
statisticians, precisely 143 books.

A few minutes on an ordinary summer's day in the Alexander-platz in East Berlin, a favoured meeting place, reveals a placid enough population. They do not have the overlay of sullenness which is so evident in Poland and Czechoslovakia. They do not dress as smartly as they do in Prague or Budapest — except in the theatres and the concert halls. In these places, the atmosphere of stiff formality — suits for the men and black dresses with lace frills for the women — can be as formidable, and as bourgeois, as anywhere in the Western world.

Possibly because of the extraordinary nature of the GDR's birth, there is a different 'feel' in the East German air compared with the air of other parts of Eastern Europe. The people's sense of humour is not the same — it is basic rather than witty — and their priorities and attitudes are not the same. Like the West Germans, but unlike most of their fellow East Europeans, many of them are at heart attached to concepts such as 'honour', 'might', 'struggle' and, inevitably, 'fatherland'.

There can be an austere, almost conservative tone in public utterances, but there is little high moralising. Erich Honecker, 'little Erich' as the satirists like to call him, does not veer off in the middle of a policy speech into sermonising as Gorbachev does in Moscow or Jaruzelski in Warsaw. In turn, people show respect to 'the authorities'. But if they are angry, as they were in 1953 and at isolated incidents since, they will react quickly and spontaneously. One winter evening in East Berlin, I watched and listened as the laughter and the catcalls for a traffic policeman who would not let the cold pedestrians cross grew and grew in intensity. Nobody, though, crossed the road before he said so.

This said, there are some laws that East Germans are quite willing to break. This book could not have been written if certain officials, some in very responsible positions, hadn't been willing on occasions to be totally indiscreet and give me their frank views on what they saw as an unsatisfactory situation. Many have taken me to their homes and many, I suspect, have not reported the fact. The subject of the conversation has frequently been in areas they and I know to be officially 'forbidden', even punishable by law.

Theoretically, everyone has the right 'to participate fully' in shaping the political, economic, social and cultural life of the country. Not everyone exercises that right, of course, though the stated turnout at elections is always said to be astonishingly high. Official demonstrations — for peace, for instance — are well attended and usually well ordered affairs, run along carefully prescribed lines. In recent years, less official demonstrations for the same cause have also been well attended, and run along equally carefully prescribed lines. The 'unofficials' were of course saying many things — but they were also expressing an important view on officialdom.

There is acute concern in high places about public apathy towards what the state is trying to achieve on the people's behalf. This applies especially in the factory where men and women from the shop-floor are delegated, by those who are interested among their fellow workers, to sit on supposedly influential 'production councils'. These delegates then find that the factory director, who is usually an SED appointment, overrules them, and that he in turn may be overruled by ministry or other state bureaucrats. Indifference and alienation can be the result.

The corollary to this situation is that the workers have the whip hand. They have the security of their jobs, after all, coupled with a virtual guarantee that unemployment does not and will not happen in the GDR. Such security, however, does not mean the worker puts more effort into his or her job — it can mean the reverse.

The arrival of Gorbachev in the Kremlin and his spreading of the gospel of perestroika and glasnost (which has not been taken up with any enthusiasm at all by the East German leadership) have led to a new irreverence from the grassroots towards the elderly policy-makers. The pressing need to know more of Gorbachev's thinking is evident from the demand for the Soviet Communist party newspaper, *Pravda*, often unobtainable in East Berlin, and the demand for his book on perestroika. I saw no sign of the book at the Soviet stall at the 1988 Leipzig Book Fair, but there were long queues (of all ages) to find out how it could be obtained.

Gorbachev's presence has given rise to a new uninhibitedness at many levels, and especially among intellectuals. They have grown less worried about being overheard and about the relative extravagance of their remarks and they relish opportunities to talk about the Soviet leader and his chances of achieving what he wants to achieve. An interesting difference between East German and other East European anti-reformers is that the East Germans do not object to Gorbachev's successes and they do not want him to fail, as is the case, I am sure, with some other well-placed ethno-centric and anti-reformist East Europeans.

There are still limits on how far even sophisticated East Germans can go in their enthusiasm for *glasnost*. The Distel cabaret in East Berlin, which plays to packed houses every night, had a whole series of sketches cancelled by the censor in 1988 for being too critical of anti-*glasnost* thinking in the GDR.

Pro-Soviet thinking has led in some quarters to a diminution of what might loosely be called 'GDR nationalism'. It could only have happened in a Warsaw Pact country in the late 1980s that a crowd of frustrated young people should converge on the Soviet Embassy, in this case in the quieter part of Unter den Linden, crying 'Gor-ba-chev, Gor-ba-chev'. It could also only be in such a country that they were quickly dispersed by the police.

One of Honecker's central dilemmas has been to reconcile this de facto erosion of nationalist pride with his own exhortations to do more for the country. At the beginning of 1989 he leaned a little towards making some concessions to the disenchanted, making it marginally easier for a few more East Germans to visit the West. Almost every East German who has not yet seen the West has an inbuilt desire to see what it is really like. From January 1989, they have been able to appeal against the bureaucratic decision to refuse a passport.

For some people in East German society, the 'state' is less burdensome than it is for others. Elites, says East German official-dom, do not exist. But look around you and the evidence of your eyes proves otherwise. They are not discussed in authorised literature or the press, but the structure of the society that has evolved over the last forty years makes their existence unavoidable.

The working class, according to Honecker, is now the ruling class and, in the sense that Honecker and his immediate colleagues are workers, this is true. But among those workers, as any honest citizen will admit, there is another group which leads an especially privileged life. This group constitutes the elite of East Germany.

The size of the elite, given the secrecy and confidentiality that surrounds it, makes total size difficult to determine. Estimates vary from two or three thousand to as much as 10 per cent of the population. But it is fair to say that people generally assumed (in the West, anyway) to constitute 'the working class' are not members unless they have been elevated, either because they 'know somebody', or because they can skilfully balance ambition with 'playing the system', or because they possess extraordinary ability or talent.

Every profession, including the profession of politics, has its crème de la crème. In the one-party system of Eastern Europe, this means a group which enjoys an out-of-the-ordinarily comfortable life-style, with perks and advantages which in the West might be taken for granted but which in the Communist area can only mean privilege.

Thus the house one lives in may be in a special 'colony' — and it may be guarded. The car at one's disposal may well be better than the two-stroke Trabant in which so many East Germans tootle around and will have become available after a very short waiting period, instead of several years. Food supplies will not be problematical because there are separate and well-stocked shops. Children have access to places in schools and colleges beyond the reach of the majority. Holidays inside the country will be in accommodation that is scrupulously appointed and looked after and, if it is outside the country, will probably be a privilege anyway. Bureaucratic hassle for this group is much less than for ordinary mortals.

Areas of activity where elites may be found are limited in number. The Socialist Unity Party, the government, the armed services, the security services, the Academy of Sciences, and recognised areas in sport and the arts are the principal ones.

So long as there are no significant upsets in the hierarchy, and given the order and discipline which hold sway in the behaviour and attitudes of the average GDR citizen, combined with the fact that a select few — a 'vanguard' — have to occupy the most senior positions, the position of these elites is secure. It is unimaginable that an East German journalist would be in a position to imitate his American or British counterpart and shout across the East German equivalent of the White House lawn or Downing Street something like 'Say, Mr Honecker, what do you think of the situation in Iran?' or 'What do you think of Romania's human rights record?'

Strategically deployed security people — not always readily identifiable, which takes them halfway to elitism themselves — surround almost every movement of the leadership of the party and the government. I once saw a very animated Honecker chatting at Schönefeld Airport, as we awaited the Gorbachevs' arrival from Moscow, but it was a very rare event.

Because East Germany is an industrialised and therefore reasonably educated society, another group has been identified — several years ago — which profits from the system. These are members of the intelligentsia who are in senior positions in middle management, or its equivalent, and who know a great deal about the system and how it works because they form the ranks immediately behind the policy-formulators, being the policy-imple-menters. These have come to be called East Germany's 'counter-elite'. ter-elite'.

They tend to belong to the younger generation, people who have made career choices since the decisive developments of 1961. They can be met in the diplomatic service, in academic circles, in the arts and the media, and in the higher echelons of the state bureaucracy. I have less often met them (outside top management) in industry.

They are realists who are also modernisers, and their strongest distinguishing mark, in my experience, is curiosity, a willingness to ask questions, to engage in argument and, interestingly, to answer searching questions as well. They have an assertive air with no chip on the shoulder (which is so often encountered in the old-guard generation) and they seem to live well and to recognise 'quality' in goods or services when they see it. Unlike their elders, they are not so obviously trying to prove something. Perhaps, indeed, they are the proof.

The Face of Dissent

'We live,' declares a dissident East German writer, 'in an authoritarian kindergarten.' It is a view held not only by dissidents, who come in all shapes and sizes and turn up in the most unlikely surroundings. It is also a view of well-placed members of the government, including party members. By and large they may feel the country is heading in the right direction, but they are not necessarily enjoying the journey.

At the end of the 1970s, a spokesperson for the authorities dismissed their critics as 'a small band of individuals who represent nothing and nobody'. It is an approach still adopted in Czechoslovakia and Romania, and until not so long ago in Poland, and it holds very little water. At this writing, the Polish Government has been bold enough to allow the opposition to run – and win – in elections to its Upper House of Parliament.

In East Germany, the line between dissidents and the rest is difficult to draw. A survey in 1983 found that a million or more skilled or otherwise qualified workers were frustrated because they could make no use of their training. A rock concert on the Western side of the Berlin Wall brought out thousands on the east side as would-be participants. A halt, in late 1988, to the circulation of the Soviet discussion magazine, *Sputnik*, had hundreds of teachers up in arms and created ferment in party cells. If the disgruntled are dissidents, then all these were dissidents.

Publicly expressed disaffection with the way the GDR is run has been evident ever since the death of Stalin in 1953. First there was the uprising of that year, and then the breakthrough de-Stalinisation speech of Nikita Khrushchev to the 20th Congress of the Soviet

Communist party in 1956, made when the new GDR was just six years old. When in 1961 Stalin's statue was pulled down in East Berlin and his name removed from public places, difficult questions began to be asked.

Robert Havemann, party member since 1932, was one of the first professors appointed to Berlin University and one of the first members of the People's Parliament. He had mourned Stalin's death as many did, but as the true facts of Stalin's rule came out, he soon began to distance himself from Stalinist perceptions. By 1962–63 he was declaring to his students that party thinkers were getting in the way of straight academic teaching of non–political subjects. By February 1964 his unusually popular lectures had been stopped, and he was expelled from the party and from university teaching. Ten years later, living in West Germany, he was unrepentant, declaring that the GDR was making a mistake in unrealistically competing with the West. He died in East Germany in 1982.

Stefan Heym, the novelist, returned to live in East Germany in 1952. He had left Germany when the Nazis came and lived for many years in the US, as an American citizen and fighting in the US Army. He wrote an account of the 1953 uprising called *Five Days in June*, but it has not yet been published in the GDR. For this and other reasons Heym became known as a square peg who would fit no round hole. His writings have been incisively critical of the regime but often in an oblique or metaphorical way — *The King David Report* was a searching analysis of politics in a totalitarian state — and he has become one of the country's most sought–after writers. He and Honecker have crossed swords on a number of occasions — Honecker fining Heym and coming close to accusing him of treason; Heym persistently irreverent, determinedly Socialist in his own way, rejecting the values of what he sees as 'a scared little dictatorship'.

Rudolf Bahro, an economist and philosopher, joined the SED a year before Stalin's death, participated in early campaigns to collectivise East German agriculture, and later worked as a journalist. His observations led him to question the nature of central planning, which he rejected, the growth of bureaucracy, which he deplored, and the lack of freedom of assembly, which he also deplored. The Soviet–led invasion of Czechoslovakia led him to set down his views in his now celebrated (not in East Germany) book, *The Alternative*. In 1978 he was sentenced to eight years' imprisonment after being tried for high treason and the betrayal of state secrets.

These three men, all intellectuals of some stature and integrity, have paid the price for speaking their minds. An increasing number of younger, talented writers — Christa Wolf and Monika Maron, for instance — have managed to survive even though they have been both harshly and circumspectly critical of the society they see around them. A sort of 'creeping glasnost' is what now seems to be gaining ground among the country's creative workers. Stephan Hermlin, one of the leading intellectuals in the East German firmament, told a West German interviewer in early 1989 that, 'more than anything', the GDR needed glasnost.

The fault of dissidents in East Germany has been that they have spoken out of turn, frequently giving voice to thoughts which, if spoken in another context by a member of the leadership, would be treated with unquestioning respect. Many of them know that Mikhail Gorbachev's thoughts in large measure echo their own and that if only they could lay their hands regularly on Soviet newspapers they would find the sort of solace — a ridiculous impossibility even a few years ago! — they cannot find in *Neues Deutschland*. The message of the 'Berlin Appeal' of January 1982, which became a seminal cry for peace and a respected document for many East European dissidents, has been repeated tirelessly by both Gorbachev and Honecker in the last few years. Its fault is that it was published in the time of Leonid Brezhnev.

Many issues raised by dissidents fit into this category, and many subjects and activities which are officially taboo in today's East Germany, but which are daily exploited on West German television, are deemed acceptable in today's Soviet Union. The peace movement is extraordinarily strong, as is the women's movement, and there are calls, increasingly well co-ordinated, for multiple-candidate elections, for more freedom of movement (linked to a dismantling of the Wall) and for a revised nuclear policy following the Chernobyl disaster.

The dilemma for the authorities in this context is that they hear the cries of the dissidents but have yet to find a way of answering them. They know that many of the dissatisfied may want to go to the West and they allow a slowly increasing number to leave. They also know that those who do not leave go into 'internal exile', together forming an alternative 'scene' in art, protest songs, rock music and so on.

Culture and the arts in East Germany are a hugely complicated affair of perpetual conflict between those with the shorter view, who restrict themselves to the time and space of the forty-year-old GDR, and those with the longer view, taking in all-German history as well as developments beyond GDR frontiers. But 'culture' covers a uniquely wide field of activities, from the latest edition of the works of Karl Marx to the private thoughts of an avant-garde poet, from 'club' activities of the Free German Youth to international conferences of scientists.

An almost unlimited range of functionaries, including ministers, bureaucrats, managers and all who work with them, as well as creative artists and everyone aspiring to be engaged in the arts, are said to be in the 'culture' industry.

There is an open-ended number of ways of considering 'culture and the arts'. I have chosen three. One is the state way, potentially pompous in its attempts to be all-embracing. The second is the 'private' way which can be intensely personal as it seeks to go in the opposite direction. The third is the 'consumer' way, which means 'gala' evenings, when everybody buys, borrows or steals clothes to see and be seen in, as well as 'ordinary' concerts or plays where it is enough to be spruced up in Sunday best.

The way of the state is unashamedly political. In 1988, for instance, its exponents exhorted everybody to pull out all stops for the so-called World Decade of Cultural Development, which had just started, 'to make the world a safer place' through works of art. They also count the number of theatres for the official Statistical Yearbook, up from seventy-seven in 1951 to well over 200 nearly forty years later, the number of books and brochures appearing, up from less than 2000 titles in 1949 to more than 6500 (a total print run which went from 33 million copies to 148 million).

The private and personal way into culture and the arts is the creative way, involving only a minority of those employed in the entire industry. This is not the place to engage in critical appraisals, but many creative works being produced in the country have met with respect among wider, international audiences. Several voraciously read novelists have been in this category for a long time, and some of the country's modern painters, working on vivid and highly expressionist themes, made critics in the West sit up and take notice when their work toured in the early 1980s.

The 'consumer' way of considering culture and the arts brings out the lingering bourgeois in the East German enthusiast. Heine's *'Philister in Sonntagsröcklein'* ('Philistines in their Sunday best') are still on parade, but many people take their reading, viewing, concert-going very seriously, dressing up to the nines, promenading at the interval and nodding politely to acquaintances seen in this or that foyer or gallery. An evening at the newly reopened Schauspielhaus, used in spite of its name for orchestral and chamber concerts, reveals that concert-goers in Germany, East or West, are little different today from what they were half a century or more ago. It can also reveal the enduring popularity of such 'traditional' composers as Beethoven, Schubert and Mozart.

The Socialist Unity Party has had an erratic relationship with the arts in its forty-odd years of existence. In the early 1950s, just before Stalin's death, the call was for the then equivalent of socialist realism. This was backed up in the same mood of the times by the widely applied obligatory teaching of Marxism-Leninism and of Russian in high schools, colleges and universities.

Ten years later the official line had softened and there was a new liberalism in the air. Coupled with the reforms that were attempted at the time in the management of the economy, one can — with hindsight — talk of a brief flowering for perestroika and glasnost, GDR-style. This process meant that the limits of tolerance, of how far creative artists could go without censorship, were not clear. Seeds of dissent and disenchantment were sown. Some performers left, when they could, for the West; others simply stopped performing.

But then, six months after he became party leader, Honecker announced another 'softening' of the official line. Nothing was impermissible, he said, so long as one started from a 'firmly socialist' point of view. This led to another period of flowering — which came to an abrupt end, signalled in 1976 by the decision to deprive the poet and singer Wolf Biermann of his East German passport. When a group of often very accomplished creative artists and intellectuals protested, they too were reined in — even expelled from their union — and a new period of conflict began.

Western cultural values, which means the cultural values from West Germany (and through West Germany, from the United States) have been decisively influential in the late 1970s and throughout the 1980s. Until the arrival of Gorbachev, it could safely be said that American products, in popular music or in the cinema, for example, were much preferred to those from the Soviet Union. Since Gorbachev, this sort of simplification no longer holds water — films which have been controversial in the Soviet Union have been sought after but hardly seen, if at all, in East Germany. The Soviet film, *Repentance*, appearing in the mid-1980s and caricaturing the Stalin era, was briefly shown, heavily criticised and then withdrawn from showing in East Berlin.

For all the exhortations by the leadership, and the high-sounding principles enunciated by the state to promote artistic and cultural activity, the real highlights for young people in East Berlin in the 1980s have been concerts by Western rock groups. Such realities are a long way from the thousands of well-meaning 'events' being staged at hundreds of arts centres up and down the country 'oriented', in official language, 'to developing the socialist personality and propagating a socialist way of life.'

A potentially pressing question for the leadership is whether it can cope with the alternative socialism that seems to be evolving. The Rosa Luxemburg slogan demanding 'freedom for those who think differently' landed those who carried it through the streets (on the anniversary of her death in 1988) in deep trouble, and some of them in prison — but it was Rosa Luxemburg nevertheless. It was the biggest operation by the authorities against 'dissent' for more then ten years.

A former party member I know was a victim of that operation. She is now a student of theology and has another slogan on her sitting room wall for comfort. It is a quotation from Mikhail Gorbachev to the effect that there is no alternative to reform. It was given to her by an evangelical minister working in East Berlin.

Bishops, priests and other religious leaders in East Germany talk quite often in terms of the tightrope they have to walk in what can be very strained dealings with the State. They have to temper their enthusiasm for what is desirable with what is achievable. One priest I met in his study in East Berlin — it was a run-down part of the city and the staircase to his room creaked alarmingly as if it was on the point of collapse — put his finger to his lips when I asked certain questions. To answer them frankly, he said later, would not have been helpful to anyone.

In January 1988, at an East Berlin cinema, there were a number of tightropes about and many people were on their best balancing behaviour. But nobody referred to them, and they might as well have been invisible. It was, to put it mildly, a sensitive occasion.

The screening was a gala showing for a new production from the German Film Company (DEFA), a film entitled *Let Each of Us Carry the Other's Burden*. The party politburo and the central committee were heavily represented, as were the government and the different denominations of the church. All sat in silence as they watched this new account of the development of the relationship between Marxists, represented by a people's police inspector, and the Christians, represented by an evangelical prelate. The message was that each side should recognise and carry out a joint responsibility for life and for people.

The 'Church from Below', a body within the Evangelical Church which seeks reform from the grassroots up, was not asked to send a delegate to the gala evening. Two days after the film was shown, it launched its own campaign for what it called 'necessary public dialogue' between church and state. The move was in protest against the continued harassment of church members who had been detained after a demonstration demanding the right to 'think differently'. Referring to those who had been arrested some days before for parading under just such a slogan on the anniversary of Luxemburg's death, the Church from Below said it was an attempt to label practising Christians as 'criminals'.

The Church from Below, significantly, wanted more freedom to hold services of intercession and of prayer. In expressing this wish, they underlined the differences that are emerging in strained times between committed Christians and others who use the church for more secular reasons. The latter are people who wish to leave the GDR and seem to think a cloak of Christianity might disguise their intentions.

About half of the country's population is nominally Protestant (evangelisch) and a little under 10 per cent is Catholic. Talk to representatives of either of them and they will tell you they have never been busier. Literally thousands turn up at some churches to take part in their services. The appeal of the church in this part of Germany has never been 'broader' than it is today; the formation, in early 1989, of an association for 'free thinkers', which would support the SED, implied the church was strong.

The clergy are concerned to have more flexibility in the teaching of religion in school, more freedom from censorship to print, circulate and read the literature they want to read, and less discrimination against practising Christians. Smaller groups that have now attached themselves seek to leave the GDR, to promote – arguing against the Soviet intervention in Afghanistan – the cause of peace and disarmament, and a cleaner environment. Members of the state security service have tried to infiltrate their meetings, but they have generally been spotted and frozen out. However, the police have been able to discover the whereabouts of 'illegal' literature on ecology, held in the precincts of a Berlin church, and to remove whatever offended them. The 'offence' was caused by the fact that such politically contentious material was being kept, and apparently used, in the precincts of a place of worship.

There are members of the church who refuse to differentiate in their attitudes between secular and spiritual work. In doing so, they point out that Martin Luther, a figure much respected by the Honecker leadership, was also one who brought the secular and spiritual together. Many others, however, seem unclear about what part the church could, and should, play. But however much confusion there may be in the minds of church leaders, the churches are well-patronised and are an important forum for public debate.

Honecker has sought through careful publicity to make much of his relationship with the church. He met church leaders for what his publicists called an 'important' meeting in early 1978, and repeated the process ten years later. At the latter meeting he emphasised that there had been a widening of the common ground between the two sides, most notably in the pursuit of peace. He spoke of the 'generally good' development of church-state relations, as he saw them, and said: 'Through their daily good work and in public life, millions of Christian citizens help to enhance the appeal of Socialism in the GDR.' Bishop Werner Leich, head of the Association of Evangelical Churches, did not reply to this rather pregnant remark, but he did thank the party leader for receiving him.

The need for each other's support, if not the precise willingness to carry each other's burden, was first clearly recognised when the 1978 meeting was held. After the relative intolerance of the Ulbricht era, that meeting led to a new formalisation of relations. Bishop Albrecht Schönherr wrote for *Neues Deutschland*, and approval was given for the construction of four new churches (mainly with West German money). Suddenly, authorisation was given for the broadcast of services and religious information on television and radio. A couple of years or so later, the World Council of Churches held a summit in the city of Dresden.

Church attitudes to peace, and specifically to the leadership's policies in this area, may be clear enough to the leadership, but inside the church they have led to confusion. The State preaches that weapons are necessary for peace; the church preaches for peace without weapons. While the state seeks to keep the environment as an issue out of the pulpit, the church smiles quietly at the success of its swords into ploughshares campaign.

One uncomfortable thorn in the State's side in the late 1980s has been Gottfried Forck, Protestant Bishop of Berlin-Brandenburg. He has declared that the church should stop at nothing in the public arena, and should not shrink from putting forthright views on political and social issues. Criticism of deplorable situations in GDR society, like the utterings of dissidents, should be seen as positive contributions, he says. Only when conditions improve in the country will people no longer want to emigrate. It is a point with which no one in the leadership could argue.

There are a host of smaller churches and religious groupings within the evangelical ambit. These include Methodists, Old Lutherans, Old Catholics, Seventh-Day Adventists, Quakers and

Mormons. All, according to officials in East Berlin, have the same legal and practical opportunity to carry out their activities.

The other large group is, of course, the Catholic church, which embraces about 1.2m. of the population, mainly concentrated around Erfurt and Dresden. Officials in (Protestant) East Berlin say there are about 300 priories and monastic communities in the country, attached to thirty-five different orders. Most of their members are nuns. Given the enormous strength of the Catholics in neighbouring Poland, where at least eight out of every ten are regular churchgoers who have often turned their back on the State, it is not surprising that East German Catholics, too, have little part in public argument.

The Jewish community in the entire country, which in the early 1930s could almost be counted in millions, is today counted in hundreds. The state leadership used to say it had no responsibility for Nazi crimes, but under Honecker, and after pressure from the world Jewish lobby, that has changed. By the end of 1988, the president of the World Jewish Congress, Mr Edgar Bronfman, had been invited to the GDR, by its Foreign Minister and was engaging in heart-to-heart talks with Erich Honecker. The latter insisted, though not all East Germans would agree, that the struggle against anti-Semitism, like the struggle against racisim, was built into GDR traditions of anti-fascism. The meeting was a minor coup for both sides.

The general thaw in East-West relations in the late 1980s was accompanied by a proliferation of organisations claiming to be concerned about human rights. In Western Europe, they tended to be multi-national in character and possibly underwritten with large sums of corporate money. In Eastern Europe, they grew on the slenderest of resources out of people's sitting rooms, triggered by a concern for individuals unjustly treated by the security authorities or the courts. In East Germany, church halls were preferred to sitting rooms.

Human rights nowadays are in the eye of the politically motivated beholder. As Mikhail Gorbachev has encouraged public discussion in the Soviet Union about wider democratisation, 'free' enterprise and relaxation of censorship, so Western pressure groups have homed in on issues like 'freedom', 'democracy' and 'repression'.

The GDR, not being reformist in the Gorbachev way, has been dubbed conservative and hard-line.

Perceptions of human rights in East Germany have almost invariably given prominence to the Wall and 'the wish to travel'. The former has become 'the wall of shame' in the eyes of the West and 'a protective barrier' to the regime which built it. There is no meeting of minds. Only those East Germans who have spent all their conscious lives 'behind' it, knowing the realities of their day-to-day living as well as the realities presented to them daily on Western television, see it in a less strident way.

In his speech-making in the 1980s, the decade of human rights and of his own conciliatory trips westward, Erich Honecker spoke frequently of what he called the people's happiness. His tone was that of someone making an honest offer which could not be refused, exuding confidence in the achievement of the country and the record of the ruling SED. The supreme principle of the party, he declared in late 1988, was 'the well-being and the happiness of the people'.

Occasionally, there has been the enforced deportation of a political 'undesirable' to West Berlin or West Germany — not always popular with the victim despite the supposedly large number who like just such a move. But no one in East Germany, as one friend pointed out to me recently, faces enforced exile to Siberia and nobody, so far as is known, is knowingly abused or mistreated in psychiatric units. There has been some mistreatment, but no torture, in East German prisons.

According to a Church survey carried out during 1988, nineteen people out of twenty do not want to emigrate, and in many people the 'need' to travel is almost irrational in character. It is a finding on which church and state just might agree.

In July 1987 the GDR became the first Warsaw Pact member country to abolish the death penalty. At the same time, the Council of State announced its latest amnesty, affecting all prisoners except those 'convicted of Nazi or war crimes, crimes against humanity, espionage and murder'. On the estimates of West German human rights activists, it was expected to affect as many as 2000 'political prisoners'. Details of the amnesty came just two days after the official announcement that Honecker would finally be making his trip to Bonn. It was a useful move to make at such a juncture.

Early in 1989, Amnesty International announced in an unusually substantial report on the GDR, published in London, that 'secret trials, secret directives to lawyers and vaguely defined laws make it possible for the authorities to penalise almost any activity of which they disapprove'. The secretiveness, according to Amnesty, was such that ordinary GDR citizens no longer knew whether or not they were breaking the law.

East German officials to whom I spoke on the day the report was published were puzzled, and slightly pained, by its message, but they remarked that it had not taken note of the new regulations for intending Grenzgänger (effective from January, 1989). Amnesty itself, on the other hand, also stated that GDR officials were reluctant to disclose information.

These regulations meant in fact that a wider range of family members would be able, for the first time, to visit relations in West Berlin and in the Federal Republic, and a wider range of reasons for making such trips could now be used by the would-be traveller. More important, however, was the provision that people refused permission to travel could demand to know the official reason why and, if they were told something improbable, they would be able to lodge an appeal. It was thus in the perennially sensitive 'wish-to-travel' area that the GDR state monolith had been broken in unprecedented style.

Pinning Down Facts

One autumn evening, as I walked down Unter den Linden in search of a favoured bookshop, I was accompanied by a colleague from an East German provincial newspaper. His specialisation was writing about the economy. He was very earnestly hammering home a message which, in his eyes, I totally failed to understand. 'You must see,' he said emphatically, 'that economics is what Socialism is all about in this country. It is performance that matters.'

The exchange was mildly frustrating, because in any discussion about the East German economy provable points can be thin on the ground. Essential facts and figures are hard to come by. Selected statistics are ritualistically given on a regular basis, but are no help if one seeks a precise and accurate picture of what has been achieved and what is projected. Some Western monitors of the GDR scene — with political axes to grind — claim the given figures are intended to deceive. Whether this argument is strengthened or not by the fact that the same figures are advanced by the leadership in keynote speeches is open to question.

It should be a problem, but it doesn't seem to be, that both the National Economic Plan and the State Budget, once nodded through by the People's Parliament, are legally binding on management and staff alike. The number of managers put on trial for breaking these laws is untraceable and the number of government ministers reshuffled out of sight as a result of illegality is non-existent. The Prime Minister, Willi Stoph, was one of the Party's chief economic policy-makers even before the GDR was formed, and at this writing had been Prime Minister for most of the last twenty-five years.

'The economic strategy of our party,' Erich Honecker told the 1986 Party Congress, 'covers the period up to the year 2000 and is designed to combine the advantages of socialism still more effectively with the achievements of the scientific and technological revolution which has entered a new phase.' To this end, he added, the politburo had adopted 'mould-breaking resolutions'. The GDR was after all unable to set its own pace. 'We will have to succeed in this race against time.'

The thousands of committed delegates to Congress who rose to their feet to applaud Honecker at the end of his day-long peroration — an astonishing performance for a man of his age — were not to know that growth rate targets would not be met in the two ensuing years. The recorded achievement in 1987 was a 4 per cent growth, the lowest for five years, and below the projected target. Even that figure, according to sceptical Westerners, is twice as high as it should be.

If scapegoats were hunted and found, they were not explicitly named. The gossip over drinks in East Berlin among the bureaucrats most closely involved was more intense than usual but lacked a focus. However, the laws for the rest of the Five-Year Plan, running until 1990, were rewritten, and the output targets lowered for the rest of its span. Cuts were made in defence spending, echoing cuts made in the Soviet Union and elsewhere in Eastern Europe.

One view in the late 1980s was that failures to meet plan targets, and shortages in the shops, could make radical change easier to implement when Honecker goes. However, at the end of 1988 Honecker himself was at it again, this time warning that capital spending was failing to meet expectations, that deliveries were not meeting promised dates, and that supplies for the long-suffering consumers were not getting through.

The biggest problem confronting those who seek to execute the plans, however unrealistic, is that their freedom of movement is limited. The rigidity of the central plan is something that many in management and in research are unhappy about. Their unhappiness deepens as they read of new avenues that seem to be opening up for management in Gorbachev's Soviet Union. But in spite of 'mould-breaking resolutions' in the politburo, the plan seems for the time being to be immutable. In the now celebrated words of politburo member Kurt Hager, the fact that the Soviet Union was 'changing its wallpaper' did not mean the GDR had to do the same.

Senior managers in East Germany are usually party members or have been approved by the party. They are unlikely to kick too hard against the pricks, however much reason they may have for doing so. In industry, for instance, much of the machinery is obsolete, giving rise to an alarming number of industrial accidents and an uncontrollable wastage of time on repairs and maintenance. Where machinery is up-to-date, computerised even, there can be shortages in available software, in sophisticated spare parts, or simply in personnel to operate it. On the farm, conditions are similarly often far from ideal. When the population refuses to grow, the deployment of sensitive workers can be a critical matter.

When the GDR came into being, it occupied an area which in pre-war days had approximately a third of Germany's total population and was producing up to a third of its industrial output. The loss of key workers during and after the war was substantial, as was the loss of machinery and equipment either as a result of war damage or the enforced reparations. There was no economic Marshall Aid for the GDR. To have reached, for however short a time, the status of one of the world's top ten industrial nations, as the GDR did in about 1970, was a huge achievement by any standards. It was, said some, a second German 'economic miracle'. To be slipping back in an age of demanding technology — and rigid central plans — may be understandable.

Some of the problems that have perennially confronted Honecker have been peculiar to East Germany. Others will sound familiar in most capitals of Eastern Europe. In the first category, there has always been the West German factor, with the leadership, bureaucrats and managers perpetually looking over their shoulders and comparing their own less sparkling performance with that on the other side. Despite big increases in output in the GDR, West German levels have in many areas remained beyond reach. Despite the innumerable research ideas that are swirling around, the technology gap — between conception and execution on the assembly line — remains increasingly unbridgeable.

Among the more generally recognisable problems, the East

Germans worry about industry's inclination to use too many raw materials, especially energy, in the manufacturing process; about the bureaucracy's over-zealousness in interfering or obstructing the production and distribution process; and about the latent unpredictability of the work-force. The workers' response is that they cannot throw everything they've got into the cause of a party which is not ready to listen when they try to explain about aspects of their living and working conditions.

Trade did not receive priority treatment in the Ulbricht era. This was understandable; the needs on the home front were paramount. But as soon as trade did take off, the aim was to make the GDR as far as possible indispensable to the Soviet Union as a trading partner. By 1985, the Russians were responsible for around 40 per cent of GDR trade turnover, with total exchanges amounting to nearly three times the total for the rest of Comecon. But when Gorbachev came to East Berlin in 1986 it was clear that the Soviet Union was becoming a very demanding customer, seeking more advanced technology and better-quality goods.

The problem of hard currency debts is one which did not bother Ulbricht very much but which assumed serious proportions under Honecker. At the beginning of 1987, the net figure owing to Western creditors was between £4 billion and £5 billion, not as high as Hungarian or Polish figures but not quite compatible with the image of efficiency and achievement that many East Germans seek, still, to promote. Here, and elsewhere, it is agreed by many in the bureaucracy, radical remedial action may be taken when Honecker departs. A re-ordering of priorities, it is felt, could ease the painful situation in this and a number of other areas.

East Germany's economic priorities have traditionally been in manufacturing and heavy industry. Its service industries, particularly its tourist industry, are still in their infancy. Tourism clearly has a future — the country is full of history, beauty and very hospitable people — but there are complications attending its growth. How do you reconcile enforceable laws on the passing of information with the need for bed and breakfast accommodation and more informal contacts? How do you stop people talking to one another and, even on holiday, touching on 'sensitive' topics? How can guests feel relaxed if their host or hostess is not?

Socialism in the second half of the twentieth century has thrown up issues undreamt of by Marx or Engels. The challenge they offer, however, has been taken up with lukewarm enthusiasm by the State. In many cases, the energy to pursue them has come from outside the party and government establishment.

Pollution and the environment is such an issue. Provisions were written into the first constitution of 1949 entitling the population to clean surroundings. It was more than twenty years, however, before comprehensive laws in this area were passed, and even when they were enforced, the GDR was still left (for example) with totally unsatisfactory water supplies. A lot of research is going on, but the implementation of sane measures is often left to the local authorities. Their relationship with offending industrialists, when it comes to pollution, is inevitably strained. When villagers are exhorted to 'Mach mit' ('Join in') and beautify their immediate surroundings, their response can be very mixed.

Much has been achieved. The Free German Youth organisation is given the credit for initiating a 'healthy forests' campaign, involving the clearing and replanting of forests. More than 100,000 acres of former mining land have been recultivated, and a number of disused open-cast sites have been converted for leisure use. One at Senftenberg, near Cottbus, has been turned into a very popular lido.

Dust emission is a big problem. Every five-year-plan includes provisions to cut dust and sulphur dioxide emissions – though these, it has to be admitted, are implemented with more than half an eye on the scope for increased productivity. Rivers and lakes, if they aren't already filthy, are threatened with pollution from industrial effluent and agricultural chemicals, but progress in remedying the situation has been hampered by disagreements between government and industry. Pollution of the Baltic Sea has made it unsafe for bathing at a number of points along the coast, and dozens of separate research projects have been started. Sewage treatment is still being developed and the biggest plant went on stream north of Berlin in 1985. This has proved a lucrative venture: much of the sewage treated – for a hard-currency fee – is from West Berlin.

Nuclear power and its further development is worrying

pressure groups. The impact of the Chernobyl disaster, and the ensuing political and radioactive fallout, has rattled the GDR government; but the commitment to nuclear power, as 'the most important alternative' to coal power, remains total. Officials claim with a straight face that nuclear power in the GDR is 'risk-free' with strict safety standards enforced.

For the time being, more than 80 per cent of the country's electricity still comes from lignite — the acrid-fumed brown coal — and slightly over 10 per cent from nuclear sources. Open-cast mining devastates great tracts of countryside and the 'acid rain' which it leads to is an acute embarrassment. The possibility of as much as 50 per cent of all electricity coming from nuclear power in the next generation or so has done little to subdue the 'green' lobby that has been emerging only a short distance behind its fashionable counterparts in the Federal Republic.

Party, East and West

In every capital of Eastern Europe, and East Berlin is no exception, the busiest public building is always the quietest. An austere armed guard or two stand in a huge doorway, scrutinising the credentials of everyone who seeks to cross their path. Behind them, a cavernous interior has a cold elegance of line but a strange emptiness, relieved perhaps by a great mural of the working class at work at one end. There are few people about. An anonymously-suited official walks through with a heavy brief-case, or an expressionless secretary heads from one room to another with yet another piece of closely-typed paper.

This building is the headquarters of the Central Committee of the ruling Communist Party — in the case of the GDR, the Socialist Unity Party (the SED). It is the nerve centre and think-tank for all policy-making in the country. On the front façade, nearly two storeys high, is the shaking-hands crest of the SED, signifying the Communists and the Social Democrats coming together. Otherwise it is the façade of the refurbished and extended Central Bank of the Third Reich. Hitler himself, in other words, provided a head office for the Party he most loved to hate.

Very slowly, but perceptibly, SED membership has been falling in recent years. Even so, on 1 January 1989 the total stood at 2.26 million members, well over one in eight of the entire population. This group of people, according to the party programme (of 1976), represents 'the politically conscious and organised vanguard' of the workers. It seeks 'unswervingly' to do all it can for the good of the general population, and its ultimate goal is 'the construction of a communist society'.

However, the vision has been tempered in the mid-1980s by unwished-for intrusions of reality. Total membership has increased considerably since it was 1.6 million in 1961, but party members have been leaving of late at the rate of 1000 and more each week, not just because of death, but latterly also because they have been angered by or tired of the continuing resistance to 'new-wave' reforms coming from Moscow. They have resented the centrally decreed unwillingness to engage in public self-criticism, to see the need for fundamental change. Of course, others have been found who have come forward and who nearly fill the places vacated by departing members, but overall numbers are still falling.

In the late summer of 1985, every single member of the party was hauled in for 'frank and confidential discussions' about where he or she, and the party, stood on the issues of the day. This happens from time to time, but on this occasion the date was significant. It was a few months after the accession in Moscow of Mikhail Gorbachev, and attitudes had to be clarified. The upshot was much argument about Honecker's leadership, but in the end a consensus that members should work still harder to promote the Honecker line.

The 'discussions' were particularly fraught with staff at the Ministry of State Security (the 'secret' police). They sought more powers from the party to deal as they see fit with 'subversive activities' and were in turn burdened by the party with 'more demanding requirements'. The ministry men said they would do all they could to help. The People's Police, meanwhile, who wear uniforms and are more visible, were patted on the back and told to keep up their good work. The GDR is one of the most rigorously policed states in Europe.

Conclusions drawn from these discussions were not exactly heartening for the young and aspiring party member. Motivation, it was found, was lacking, and there had to be more imagination and resourcefulness in meeting public needs. The 'climate of trust', which is liable to be weakened by incipient apathy, scepticism and cynicism, had to be strengthened. The 'masses' needed convincing — still — that the SED had their interests at heart, and one answer to this was to improve standards within the party itself. Cell meetings would have to be more purposeful.

It is hard, on reading such a candid report of these discussions, to escape the feeling that for some the party was apparently running out of steam, that for large sectors of the population it had lost credibility. Nobody, it is well known, reads the party slogans festooned about the factory walls or the city streets anywhere in Eastern Europe any more, and party meetings which do not discuss the questions thrown up by reform can be deadly dull. 'Karl Marx actually died in 1883,' an East German friend who is a card-holder told me in 1988. 'We are now in the age of high-tech, heading for the year 2000 with a bucket and spade.'

The social make-up of the party is interesting. Every third member is an intellectual, a white-collar worker or a student; every seventh member is an old age pensioner; nearly three out of every five are (unspecified) 'workers'. Roughly one in six has a university degree, and every other one is said to have attended an approved party course (minimum duration three months). The average age of all members is between forty-four and forty-five; significantly, the average age of the ruling politburo is twenty years higher.

The Free German Youth (FDJ) organisation, which prepares young people for a political way of thinking, has a membership of around 2.3 million, which means that about three out of every ten boys and girls don't want to know. For the leadership, the FDJ plays a pioneering role in bringing the party's new ideas to fruition. Watching an FDJ parade march rather jauntily down Unter den Linden one afternoon in early 1986, I couldn't help feeling they did so with a touch of irreverence. And how symptomatic was it that they left an inordinate amount of litter in the most elegant thoroughfare in the city?

There is acute sensitivity among thinking members of the SED about the party's past and about the history of Communism in general. As with all other ruling parties, memories have to be selective on 'difficult' issues and the agreed party line on a given matter or personality can be difficult to determine, and can vary with the passage of time. Thus, Marx and Engels, not least because they were Germans, remain more or less irreproachable in every respect — though there were deep disagreements in party committee rooms about how they should be commemorated. The relatively small statue now in the centre of the city was a long time coming and is smaller than many expected for such epoch-making figures.

There is a certain ambivalence, too, towards Karl Liebknecht and Rosa Luxemburg. Each year when the anniversary of their murders comes round there are speeches from the politburo, but there is still no statue to either of them. Since these two were central to the founding of the German Communist Party (the KPD), it is a strangely conspicuous omission. And when unofficial demonstrations are held by young people bearing banners and slogans of some of Luxemburg's less tractable thinking, they are quickly brought to an end.

The memory of Ernst Thälmann seems to be safe. He was honoured with the unveiling of a huge sculpture of his bullish head in 1986, and a park and a housing estate have been named after him. He was not a great or original thinker, but he was a leader who did what Moscow told him and he died a martyr's death in a Nazi concentration camp.

Walter Ulbricht has presented more of a problem. He was single-minded to the point that in some of his own staff's eyes he appeared dictatorial when he lived. On some matters of importance and public interest he would brook no discussion. He died under a cloud and there were disagreements over what sort of funeral he should have. He was barely mentioned for several years afterwards. By the mid-1980s, however, there was change of emphasis: he was after all the figurehead in the GDR's most difficult and trying years. He was reassessed. But feelings are so mixed about him that a statue still seems a long way from materialising.

In years to come, Honecker could have similar problems. No one claims all his policies have met with unanimous approval all the way along the line. Many in the party have indicated that a younger man should have taken his place long ago. A statue for him too could be a long time in coming.

Early in 1989, the country which owes its existence to Stalin more than any other individual, and a leadership which owes its position to all he stood for, was at last coming to terms with realities. Some realities were evidently more acceptable than others and not everything that was being said and printed in the Soviet

Union in the ultimate de-Stalinisation campaign of 1988 has been deemed acceptable. Nor, on the other hand, was it publicly acknowledged until 1988 that the same Stalin who made Thälmann, Ulbricht and, indirectly, Honecker, had also liquidated several hundred German Communists in the period immediately before the Second World War.

Until 1988, it was more or less routine for questions about Stalin's purges and 'executions' of non-conforming German party members to be ignored and avoided. The SED swept these things under the carpet and out of public view. With Gorbachev's decision to allow access to the archives, held in Moscow, of the Communist International, however, everything changed. Demands from academics and students in East Berlin for 'the truth' are being acceded to with painstaking vigour. It is clear that when the researches are complete, many East German 'victims' will have to be posthumously rehabilitated.

In the same month — December 1988 — that I reported on the explosive nature of these researches, Honecker addressed an important meeting of the party's Central Committee. 'The triumph of socialism,' he told them very pointedly, 'does not depend on wishful thinking ... The GDR is not an Island of the Blessed and it must not be surrounded with an aura of infallibility.'

In the other Germany, meanwhile, against the background of Europe's most vigorous capitalist economy, there exists one of Western Europe's smallest Communist parties. The West German Communist Party (the DKP) is notionally a mirror image of the East German SED but it is so inconsequential in its deliberations and its electoral achievements — which are currently nil — as to shatter for ever any dreams that either side might cherish of a unified socialist Germany. It should on no account be confused with the mighty KPD of the pre-Nazi era.

A congress of the West German Party, held in Frankfurt in early 1989, found the leadership admitting that it was in the throes of a serious crisis. In the presence of Hermann Axen, an East German politburo member for more than twenty years, and Alexander Yakovlev, a 'new' Communist from the Gorbachev camp in Moscow, delegates heard Herbert Mies, their chairman, urgently appeal for unity. He did so because, as he acknowledged, the party had made mistakes. It was also deeply divided over how far to go in support of *perestroika* and *glasnost* (Yakovlev) and how far to go in resisting it (Axen). There were twelve hours of fierce argument behind closed doors. Either way, it did not look as though it would be a completely happy DKP guest at the GDR's fortieth birthday celebrations later in the year.

By implication, it might be thought that the East Germans had great faith in the West German comrades. There is a membership of between 50,000 and 60,000, compared with around 20,000 when it was founded in 1969. Present membership is broken down into about 1000 local groups or 'cells' scattered around the country. In addition, there are about 500 groups in factories and offices, many in the Ruhr valley and other industrial areas. Membership includes a preponderance of older, more stick-in-the-mud elements — some of whom have been supporters from the moment the party resurfaced a few weeks after the end of the Second World War. The Socialist Unity Party in West Berlin (the SEW) has about 8000 members.

East German support is essential for both the West German and the West Berlin Communist parties to survive. There are large infusions of cash, plus training courses for willing students, holidays for young people and literature on issues of the day. Given the recognisable split in members' loyalties, a survey of the actual interest taken in the GDR offerings, in the 'take-up' by the members, would be very revealing.

The anomaly is that the two parties' predecessor, the Communist Party of Germany (the KPD) which was formed seventy years ago, was in its heyday the biggest party in Europe. Even after the war, when a clearly pro-Stalin position was being adopted, membership was in the region of 300,000. But then a series of steps led to a vitiation of that number: the expulsion of 'Titoist' elements, arguments for and against the formation of the Federal Republic and the adoption of a generally pro-Stalin stance during the first Cold War years.

Then, as East Germany became recognisable as chief patron, there were the self-inflicted shootings in the foot. There was a hard line from the West German Communists in support of the suppression of the 1953 uprising in Berlin, and there were calls for revolution to overthrow the administration of Konrad Adenauer. The old man replied by outlawing the West German party overnight, barring party members from state employment, and putting on trial several thousands of its allegedly more subversive elements. Many left West Germany to settle in the GDR.

Going underground — which was nothing new to socialists in Germany — meant the KPD setting up a provisional headquarters in East Berlin and accepting Walter Ulbricht's munificence when party congresses were held in 1957 and 1963. The self-inflicted wounds, however, continued: there was total and unsubtle support (in a highly charged emotional atmosphere) for the building of the Berlin Wall and a similar lack of equivocation over the Soviet-led invasion of Czechoslovakia in 1968.

There was no sympathy either with even the most celebrated East German dissident and, in 1980–81, there was no sympathy with Solidarity in Poland. Given the climate of the times, this was not a way to make friends and influence people.

But when the newly formed DKP came up from underground again in 1969, it discovered that its biggest tragedy had happened behind its back. The 1960s had seen pressure groups and interest groups mushroom throughout Western Europe, and West Germany was in the forefront of this process. New groups formed to oppose nuclear power, to oppose the US presence on West German soil, to argue for a less polluted environment and for more sexual freedom, had effectively stolen the clothes of West Germany's Communists. They had drawn young idealists and many cerebral members away from the banned party.

The party's own reaction has been one of little more than disappointment, followed by gentle persuasion. Its methods are not aggressive, partly because its predecessors burned their fingers in the mid-1950s. It has even professed as a body not to be unduly concerned by those who now call themselves Greens or Alternatives.

Given the confusion that now exists as a result of Gorbachev's thinking, the party in West Germany can be seen as simultaneously ossified in its thinking, but fractured, if not split, in several places. Only the moral support and visible muscle power of youth protest groups who are loosely associated with it, as well as East German funds, have kept them ideologically and financially buoyant.

The DKP announced early in its new life that what it sought was 'real political democracy for the people'. For many West Germans, even of a soft left persuasion, that formula was something the country had already implemented. Willy Brandt, who was then Chancellor, may have had faults, they said, but he did profess to be a democrat. Twenty years on and there has been little dynamic movement from the DKP. The East German Party may be starting a new life at forty, but for its unpredictable foster child in the West, the prognosis does not seem to be good.

Social Security and the Other Kind

Until the mid-1980s success in a Socialist society was generally measured, by the leaders and often by outsiders as well, in terms of economic performance. Under the twin impact of world recession and then Gorbachev's new thinking, there have had to be adjustments to these criteria. Adjustments were made earlier and more emphatically in East Germany, partly to encourage people to believe in the GDR as a homeland and not to pine for the grass which appears greener in the Federal Republic next door.

In the Ulbricht era, the emphasis of early investment programmes was in industry. No one says it quite explicitly today but there had to be something, in the manufacturing and production sectors, to replace what was being removed by the Soviet occupiers. Housing tended to be neglected in the GDR's early years and the provision of welfare facilities was not something that figured very highly in Ulbricht's thinking.

Under Honecker the shift has been decisive. Plans and promises to improve a grievous housing situation have come with refreshing regularity in almost every important domestic policy speech. People who had thought of leaving the country and newly-weds who despaired of ever living a self-contained life sat up and took notice. By the end of the 1980s, Honecker was declaring that housing 'as a social problem' would be solved by 1990 — though the detail of this thought is not quite clear to the naked eye.

In Honecker's first five-year plan period — up to 1975 — more than 600,000 homes were built or modernised; in the second, more than 750,000; in the third and fourth, if targets are to be met, there would have to be another 1,650,000. The feeling of observers of the scene in early 1989 is that the shot at the 1990 goal will be a near miss, which in the central planning context is commendable. A little over 10 per cent of the total will be privately built.

Even so, young couples still have to wait several years for their first home. On statistical evidence, it has a more than even chance of being without central heating, a one-in-three chance of being without running hot water, and a one-in-four chance of being without an inside lavatory. The rent, however, will be extremely low — around 6 per cent of the worker's average wage. The space, in terms of square feet per person, will also be markedly less than it is in West Germany, and there is a fifty-fifty possibility that it will be in a refurbished older building rather than a new one.

The young married couple are entitled to preferential loans to help them to convert their dwelling into a home, and even to buy essential furniture. The unmarried couple may find it more difficult to obtain such entitlements, because the state prefers them to be legally wed. Abortion is legal, but in the event of pregnancy the woman knows that she will get a year's paid leave from work for her first child as well as a lump sum and the promise of her job back.

Health care is up to the standards of industrialised societies, especially in the bigger cities. Remoter country areas tend to be the losers. Overall, there are just over 100 hospital beds for every 10,000 members of the population, higher than the West European average and much higher than the East European average. At the same time, there is one doctor for every 411 East Germans, which is a 50 per cent improvement on the 1970 figure, and one dentist for every 1328, which is a 75 per cent improvement on 1970.

There are an unusually high number of pensioners in East Germany, measured against the number who are working. It is a fact which becomes readily apparent in any shopping precinct. The workers are at work and the four pensioners out of five who no longer work (officially) are easily identified, either diligently scouring shops for what is available, or child-minding.

The best-off pensioners are those who were in the most cosseted areas of employment — the Army, the police, some of the professions and bureaucracies. Their pensions tend to be higher than the average and the perks and facilities to which they have access correspondingly more beneficial. Pensioners known to have been imprisoned or tortured or to have otherwise suffered under the Nazis receive extra benefits.

Expectation of life seems to be marginally higher in East Germany than it is in West Germany, and it is interesting to compare the incidence of certain illnesses between East and West Germany. Tuberculosis is twice as prevalent in West Germany, while gonorrhoea is twice as prevalent in East Germany. Death as a result of heart trouble is much more likely in East Germany, but from cancer or associated illnesses much less likely. Death at work from industrial injuries is known to be an area of deep concern among East German officialdom, but it is not publicly discussed.

About a quarter of East Germany's population is under twenty, an age group which is a source of increasing disquiet to the authorities. Not only have some of its representatives shown in vociferous exchanges with the police that they prefer Gorbachev to Honecker and Western rock music and films to the home-made products, but they have also indicated, in surveys of opinion conducted as they left college or university, that they don't necessarily want to join the elite and they don't particularly care to be 'leaders' in tomorrow's GDR.

About half of the women graduates, according to these surveys, and almost two-thirds of the men said they would prefer to specialise, since a career in technology in today's climate would be more satisfying than a job in top management or decision-making. A good marriage and a happy family, somewhat unexpectedly, are seen as worth striving for. Well over one in four meanwhile choose not to give themselves a lift to a secure future by joining the Free German Youth organisation for aspiring young Communists, and many who do join are members in name only.

Almost all social and cultural activities, as well as those that are overtly political, which are organised for young people are with Party objectives firmly in mind. Where the organising has conflicted with the more spontaneous inclinations of the young people themselves, there has been confusion. Some years ago, one leader of the Free German Youth went so far as to admit that many members were totally out of sympathy with the objectives of the Party.

Though young people might at first seem to be the more privileged members of East German society, in fact there has been disquiet in recent years about the extent to which they have not fulfilled, or been able to fulfil, official expectations. By and large, East German school-leavers are well-trained by international standards, but they have not always been able to meet the needs of the national economy, and especially the shortage of specialists. The cry from the centre has been that their teachers have not been imaginative or innovative enough to keep pace with technological requirements.

Drugs among the young are not the problem they are in the cities of Western Europe, although it is known that some drugs are circulating. There are some seedy corners of East Berlin and of other conurbations where drugs can be found. In recent years there have been occasional cases of skinheads being brought to trial, charged with hooliganism. They have defended their behaviour with assertions that they are what they are because they are forced to live in East Germany when they would rather be elsewhere.

Alcohol, on the other hand, is a major problem. Drunkenness is not as visible as it plainly is in, for example, Poland, but consumption for every man, woman and child is put at a high 10 litres a head a year of pure alcohol or equivalent. Drink can be legally bought over the counter from the age of sixteen. Half of all juvenile crime, it has been calculated, is committed under the influence of alcohol and a campaign to prevent its abuse has been taken even into the country's schools.

Under Ulbricht, sport was encouraged among young people. One of the first public facilities built in East Berlin after the Second World War was the Walter Ulbricht stadium. He saw sport as a means, in the early days, of achieving international recognition and of building up 'national' pride. Today, there are special schools, some starting as early as seven or eight, where children with special aptitudes are intensively trained to excel. As successive Olympic Games have shown, they tend to be successful. Many young people, it should be noted tangentially, turn to sport for the unparalleled opportunities it gives for close contact with the opposite sex. Football supporters, to judge by some recent court cases, have also had opportunities for football hooliganism.

Sport follows a familiar European pattern, but participation is a serious matter. There are more than half a million known footballers, and almost as many anglers and gymnasts. There is also intense activity in table tennis, volleyball and, somewhat unexpectedly, rugby union. The seriousness derives not only from the keen competitive element, but also from the commitment and the required investment. The state, as a matter of policy, encourages sport, but it is the family that has to show perseverance and to spend hard-earned cash to sustain the commitment.

What of women in East Germany? The German woman of the future, wrote August Bebel in 1879, will be socially and economically independent. She will no longer be subjected to even a hint of domination or exploitation. She will be free and on a par with man, mistress of her own destiny.

These words appeared in his book, *Women and Socialism*, which according to today's East Germans was the most widely read work of Socialist literature in the nineteenth century after the *Communist Manifesto* of Marx and Engels. But, also according to today's East Germans, there were plenty of readers of the original Bebel who dismissed his thinking as starry-eyed, and his projections as little better than a guidebook to an unattainable Utopia.

Forty years after the founding of the GDR, no woman has yet served as a full member of the policy-making party politburo. Very few women have served as members of the GDR government and they remain, as ever, a minority in the ruling party. They are told, almost invariably by men, that they are doing very nicely and that, anyway, 'hostility towards men is absurd for women in a socialist society'.

In fact, women are discriminated against on a number of points, and long before the pay packet. Many women work as cooks, hairdressers, nursery teachers, nurses or typists, but there are few who effect an entry into the better-paid areas of mechanics or engineering. In the professions, they have made some headway: almost half the country's judges, doctors and magistrates are women, and more than half the country's chemists and dentists.

There are known to be unauthorised but active 'women's groups', in the Western sense of the words, in about a dozen East

German towns and cities. They have set up working groups devoted, unofficially, to such politically sensitive questions as peace in our time; ecology; and social issues. Quietly and unostentatiously, they also offer classes in acting, dancing, and the art of relaxation.

An unknown number of clubs for lesbians exist, and homosexuality in both sexes is tolerated and openly discussed. The incidence of AIDS is a matter of acknowledged concern — something which cannot be said for all East European countries.

Old-fashioned courtesies towards women, which are an everyday occurrence in People's Poland, for example, are a rarity in the GDR. Women in paid employment are still expected, by their menfolk, to come home and do most of the housework. Surveys have shown that however many hours the average man does 'about the house' in an average week, the average woman, or perhaps women, do six or seven times as many. Thus women have measurably less free time than men.

Nearly nine women out of every ten of working age are employed, and, of course, legalised abortion at the end of the 1970s and the increased benefits when children are born have made women's lives ostensibly easier in this direction. Facilities for small children in the kindergarten and the crèche are plentiful and extremely good. In theory, there is equal pay for equal work. Nevertheless, there is discrimination on a large scale, a sense of acute frustration among the women who are articulate (especially women novelists of the present generation), and, even among officials, there is a ready acknowledgement that things are moving too slowly.

The Democratic Women's League (the DFD) was established in early 1947, nearly two years after the war and long before the establishment of the GDR itself. Today it has a given membership of only about 1.3 million, little more than one in three of all working women. Apathy seems widespread and when the first women's congress was held in mid-1954, only 60 per cent of the delegates were League members.

In DFD literature, it is acknowledged that women are 'indispensable' to the construction of an advanced socialist society. This is true — almost exactly half the total workforce are women and the economy would collapse without them. However, little is said in the way of official consciousness-raising and women are called upon as GDR workers or citizens, rather than as women, to do their bit for the country. A woman who works means as much for society, if not more, than she does for the women's cause.

All in all, it is a male-dominated society where little real change can be expected. The impact of the unofficial women's groups has been less than dramatic. How, one friend wondered, can it be otherwise when Article Two of the GDR Constitution states quite clearly: 'Man shall be at the centre of all the endeavours of socialist society and its state'?

In the social context, there is another, very different, category of people which requires scrutiny. This is the category which wears a uniform — or, so I am not misunderstood, which *seems* to wear a uniform. It impinges very much on everyday life, and its existence leads one to the tentative conclusion that the country would be almost nowhere today if it were not for the controlling influence of such people, wearing uniforms — and enjoying wearing them. They may or may not be entitled to exercise authority over other people's lives, nevertheless they are frequently willing to exercise something very close to authority to meet the law and order requirements of a given situation. Most important, they are respected by those who do not wear uniform.

Often, of course, they are people applying an appropriate law in a given situation, but often they are applying a law which does not exist in any statute book but which seems, to the person executing it, to be viable in the circumstances. In other words they belong not only, and automatically, to the uniformed police, the Army and the frontier guards, and the 'plain clothes' security services, but also to the serried ranks of part-time militia members, petty bureaucrats, railway guards, waiters and cloakroom attendants. The man or woman at the door of a museum or art gallery, or who marshals the queue waiting for seats in a restaurant, or even a small tea shop, may be a member. It is not always easy to tell; the uniform, in a manner of speaking, is not always visible.

Given the history, and the raison d'être, of the country, the National People's Army occupies an important place in policy-making, public ceremonials and in the state budget. Defence spending, according to Western estimates, despite cuts in troop levels announced in early 1989, now runs at around £250 a head a year, the highest after the Soviet Union in the entire Warsaw Pact.

Compulsory national service, with some exceptions for conscientious objectors, was introduced at the end of 1961. The uniforms of the conscripts, seen in public places, are probably the most un-Prussian and forlorn of the whole range. Even so, the Scharnhorst Award, named after the reforming Prussian general who was born in 1755, remains the Army's highest honour. A monument to him stands in Unter den Linden.

Uniformed police are plentiful, especially in urban areas, and can be arbitrary in the exercise of their powers, stopping a driver perhaps to look over his car in a spot check, or stopping an innocent pedestrian, as happened to me during the Gorbachev visit of 1986, to examine his passport. (An encounter that ended with the policeman saying: 'Sorry to have bothered you. Have a nice day.')

Less evident, but no less effective, are the security people who do not wear an obvious uniform but have a certain look, even a certain 'smell' about them which others lack. Such people may be interpreters/companions for unknowing visitors to the country; or they may be behind international hotel counters; or they may be behind a desk, at the other end of a telephone, or on duty when a 'sensitive' East German who has been in contact with a Westerner reports back on the visiting Westerner's particular interests.

At the other end of the scale, the power exercised by uniformed waiters and waitresses is legendary. A sketch at the Distel cabaret in East Berlin which depicts an arrogant waiter and an increasingly frustrated customer is always hugely popular. Getting the better of any uniformed official or bureaucrat is one of the most enjoyable, comforting experiences of the average East German's daily round.

First and last, there is the particular type of uniformed officiousness at the country's very front door. I was held up for an hour and a half in the middle of 1988 when I attempted to take through a copy of my book on Berlin's history. Apparently officials wanted to photocopy every page.

But a brutal peremptoriness which was evident at the frontier

some years ago seems to be no longer in fashion. At Checkpoint
Charlie in the early 1970s I was once in a hurry to cross westwards
to catch a flight home when a starched and braided lady advanced
on me and chose to linger an excessively long time over searching
my luggage.

'Why,' I asked, 'do you take so long?'

'Because,' she replied coldly, 'we are proud of our frontier
services in the GDR.'

'In that case,' I said, 'may I take your photograph?'

'*Nein*,' she shouted and, almost throwing my bag at me, ordered
me to leave her territory immediately.

Germans, East & West

'Strictly speaking', Erich Honecker announced in December 1988, living standards were higher in the GDR than they were in West Germany. He did not elaborate, but it is not difficult in East Germany to get the impression that the most blatant prejudice felt in the first Socialist state on German soil is that which is acted out against the West Germans. The very people whom the East Germans would most like to overtake in so many areas of human endeavour — from the Olympic Games medals table to the table of indices for the national economy — are officially regarded with suspicion and with very mixed feelings. They may offer some diplomatic succour to the East Germans, favourable terms of life-giving trade, and kinship — but still, and especially if there is the slightest drop in the international temperature, they are treated as if they seriously wanted World War Three to start tomorrow.

Hundreds of thousands are welcomed as relatives. They bring barely concealed bundles of West German marks to spend, and they bring goods (gadgetry, spare parts, food, and so on) goodwill, and gifts which are very acceptable. But still, even at less than official level, there is suspicion and occasional resentment. According to some East German commentators, there are West Germans who are acceptable and West Germans who never cease to emphasise how they have outperformed their Eastern brothers. These are the ones who, in East German eyes, flaunt a sort of superiority complex. The game of pity which they play is regarded, however unjustifiably, with distaste, and is 'repaid' by the East Germans who exploit the West Germans by demanding hard currency for a variety of goods and services.

In the foyers of the biggest hotels in East Berlin, Dresden, Leipzig and elsewhere, the West Germans are certainly visible. They are well dressed, sometimes with what can only be described as a mischievous flamboyance. They eat, drink and often rather noisily make a point of 'enjoying themselves'. Perhaps, suggested an East German acquaintance as we watched them one 1988 evening from our leather armchairs, they are getting their own back for past Soviet 'threats' — as once perceived by Chancellor Adenauer — to take control of Western Germany.

By any standards the German–German relationship has to be construed as 'a special relationship'. Honecker, after all, was born in what is now West Germany; Hans–Dietrich Genscher, the West German statesman, was born and brought up in East Germany. The West Germans have talked off and on for decades about 'the unresolved national problem', while the East Germans, hearing only too clearly what they say, and recognising their own refrain of the late 1940s and early 1950s, have countered that no such problem exists.

The two Germanies, the East Germans claim, should deal with each other on the basis of international law, as would two 'foreign' states. Two very specific demands from East Berlin are for recognition of GDR citizenship and for the upgrading of each side's permanent missions in Bonn and East Berlin into full embassies.

Such exchanges are noted with varying measures of anguish by ordinary Germans on both sides, but they take place, as it were, over their heads. They make no difference whatsoever to the 'wish to travel', evinced by every other East German in conversation, which starts with a wish to see West Germany. Each side is intensely curious to know more, to get under the skin of the other.

Almost all East Germans are able to watch West German television every night of the week, and large numbers of them do just that. What they see can be lively and entertaining, and of a high standard. West German viewers are treated to lengthy extracts from GDR news bulletins. These tend to be informative, but overlaid with a sort of dullness. That is one level of curiosity. At another level there is what is loosely called spying, though perhaps — given that it is one German against another — prying might be a more accurate term.

The East Germans say that West Berlin bristles with centres for West German and Nato spies; the West Germans point to the glamorous secretaries to West German ministers who are uncovered as intelligence workers from time to time, and to the so-called traders who are so obviously engaged in industrial espionage and the hunt for high technology from West German sources.

Contacts and visits that are authorised between East and West are monitored meticulously. Mournful queues at the Friedrichstrasse crossing point in East Berlin provide the evidence that it is overwhelmingly pensioners who are allowed to make trips westwards with the least hindrance. However, a steadily increasing number below pension age are now being allowed to go through. Close to 40,000 East Germans of all ages emigrated to West Germany in 1988; just under 20,000 had done so in 1987, and the (West German) expectation was that as many as 60,000 might cross over in 1989. By 1989, furthermore, it was expected that only one in seven of those crossing would be pensioners.

Officials I have met in the GDR Foreign Ministry to discuss the German question have tended to be desiccated individuals, bound by the logic of their two-foreign-states argument and unwilling to concede that finer feelings may be involved. They are discomfited to some extent when I refer to East Germans who have sometimes sought asylum in West German embassies, and in missions in East Berlin and elsewhere in Eastern Europe. 'But that,' they insist, 'is a problem for the Federal Republic, not for us.'

In tune with the materialistic instincts of Europe in the 1980s, money has talked eloquently in the movement of Germans from East to West. The highly secret exchanges between Wolfgang Vogel, an East German lawyer who pays usually unspecified sums of Western marks to allow East Germans to emigrate, and operates out of a pleasant suburban house in East Berlin, and Ludwig Rehlinger, a senior West German civil servant in Bonn, have become legendary since the erection of the 1961 Wall.

As Honecker's so-called official representative for humanitarian dealings with West Germany, Vogel has 'transacted' the departure of close on 30,000 East Germans in return for an injection of around £350 million into the East German economy — though no 'official' figures are given. The morally questionable nature of these deals is said to be less apparent to those who finish up in West Germany, though the East German media make great play in their turn in talking of the misfortunes of those who go west and are unable to find a job or otherwise settle down.

The extent to which such money-for-people deals may seem demeaning to any thinking German, or even exploitative, is tempered by the growing confidence that has permeated East German officialdom in recent years. It has been especially apparent, as I see it, since Honecker visited the Federal Republic at the end of 1987. At state propaganda level it has been noticeable in the noise made since the dismantling and removal of nuclear warheads from both sides, with the West climbing down first. But there have also been, despite intermittent hiccups, improvements in some trends of the GDR economy. The two German systems, Honecker pointed out with some satisfaction during his visit to the other side, are as incompatible as fire and water.

The East German leader created more confidence in himself as a leader of some substance, a statesman even, as a result of the 1987 visit. He was received in Bonn with the sort of ceremony that heads of state expect on official visits — even though there were some minor adjustments to protocol — and he was listened to with respect by West German politicians of all complexions. He also managed to obtain new bi-lateral agreements to bring each side closer to the other in science and technology, pollution and the environment, and protection from radiation.

Germans on both sides rated the visit a success. They entered 1988 convinced that it, and the ideological agreement between the SED and the West German SPD, had broken new ground, and that as a consequence relations between the two Germanies could only improve.

Trade turnover between the two Germanies has been to the tune of several billion pounds a year for several years now, and shows no sign of declining. East Germans are happy to accept West German machinery and equipment which they use to modernise their production lines as well as petroleum and chemical products and semi-manufactures for industry. They sell to the West Germans textiles and clothing, refined Soviet oil, and also some chemical products.

West Germany is the GDR's second biggest trade partner world-wide, after the Soviet Union, but well ahead of Czechoslovakia, which is third. An additional bonus for East Germans is that they have an entrée into the Common Market and do not pay EEC tariffs. Nor do they have to pay for what they buy in hard currencies. Transactions are conducted between the two countries' central banks in special units of account. The bonus for West Germans is said to be mainly political, in the form of improved contacts and confidence-building.

Perhaps in the end it would be more accurate to say that both sides exploit each other — in the best, as well as in the less-than-best sense of the word. People's Germany has now cultivated, at the newest hotel in East Berlin, the Grand — one of the most expensive in all Eastern Europe — a new way deep into West German pockets. This is through the orchestration of a sumptuous season of luxury balls.

The autumn event goes under the exotic title of 'Une Impression de L'Automne', presenting what is promised as a dazzling array of artistic and culinary delights. Treat yourself, says the sales literature in the best Weimar tradition, to a relaxing evening in your finest clothes. The basic cost per person (mid-1988) is 300 West German marks, more or less £100 a head. Bed and board cost a great deal more.

Two years after the end of the Second World War, and a few years before his own death, a German artist, Paul Fuhrmann, painted a picture which he called 'The Face of Fascism'. It depicts a cadaverous Hitler at its centre, acknowledging the adulation of crowds at his feet while, behind his back, overfed generals and a monocled businessman toast each other in sparkling wine. Around this centre are other cameos, showing the horror of the battlefield, with ruins and corpses everywhere, and the anguish of the home front, as weeping civilians search for shelter amid the bombed-out, blazing remains around them. Other cameos show executions in a concentration camp and members of the Hitler Youth on the march.

It is not a great picture, and it carries messages that are not difficult to digest. The most loaded of these messages seems to be that Hitlerism embraced all kinds of people. No one is shown fighting against the Führer and no one is shown engaged in any activity that is not a direct consequence of Hitlerism in action. Today, the picture, which gains in strength because it is painted in such subdued colours, hangs in the GDR Army Museum in Dresden.

It encapsulates what for many years was the considered view of the country's policy-makers: that most, if not all, Germans, except perceptive Communist Party members, bear a responsibility for Nazism and that all who visit the Dresden museum should recognise the horrors that flowed from it. The implication, reinforced in almost every speech that treats even remotely the last war, is that such things must never be allowed to happen again. These at least seem, from their public utterances, to be the views of most of the GDR leadership. Ordinary citizens say nothing publicly against such sentiments, of course, though among my own acquaintance, there does seem to be a great deal of furtive curiosity about the Nazi period.

Fuhrmann is not the only artist to have portrayed Nazism after the end of the last war. Almost any exhibition of modern East German art will include pictures on the theme either of the horrors and the bestiality of the war or on the theme of peace and serenity which post-war administrations have sought to foster in their place. The most attention and the most propagandist publicity are reserved for those works which accomplish this task most vividly. Nazism is a past that the leadership has no intention of forgetting.

The year 1985, which saw the fortieth anniversary of the war's end, was ostentatiously marked in a number of ways. The first of September was designated World Peace Day, on which more than 3 million East Germans were said to have worked an extra shift. In the course of the year, hundreds of thousands of people went to the sites of the Buchenwald, Ravensbrück and Sachsenhausen concentration camps to remember those who suffered there, while similar numbers gathered for ceremonies in Dresden, Magdeburg, Dessau, Jena and other cities which were destroyed or largely destroyed in the war.

In the last three weeks of the war, dominated by the final battle for Berlin, nearly half a million German officers and men were taken prisoner and an unknown number died. More than 100,000 Soviet soldiers lost their lives in the final engagements, and the remains of 18,000 of them are buried at the memorial parks of Treptow and Pankow-Schönholz in Berlin. Treptow has now become a place of pilgrimage for Soviet dignitaries who are visiting Berlin.

All over the country there are smaller memorials to those who died in the war against Nazism. Every year there are hundreds of new books on the same subject, while theatres and cinemas include in their repertoire plays and feature films which hammer the same message home. The rituals conducted in Unter den Linden by the goose-stepping soldiers of the National People's Army each day at the Neue Wache, now the officially designated Memorial to the Victims of Fascism and Militarism, perform the same task.

Until 1988 it was the public stance of the East German leadership, several of whom served prison spells as Communists during the Nazi era, to maintain that all traces of Nazism had been expunged from East German soil and that the present administration bore no obligation to compensate those who had suffered.

In June of that year, however, after several years of pressure from the world's Jewish lobby, the East German Government indicated an agreement in principle to pay compensation. This followed a policy decision of some months before, that investment capital would be put aside for the rebuilding of the great Oranienburger-Strasse synagogue in East Berlin, ransacked and set on fire by the Nazis in the Reichskristallnacht of 1938.

Ironically, the national conscience was laid bare in 1988 in quite a different way. Five East Berlin youths were sentenced to terms of imprisonment for desecrating around 200 graves in the Jewish cemetery at Weissensee. They were said to have used the Hitler salute, to have uprooted grave stones and to have urinated on them, shouting anti-Semitic slogans as they did so. Psychologists called in to give evidence said the young people were either drunk, bored or emotionally 'degenerate'. The prosecution said they had been watching West German television films which glorified the Nazi era; others, outside the court, said the GDR line on anti-Nazism had conspicuously failed in this case.

A little deeper probing by one East German newspaper expressed consternation that one of the youths — aged just sixteen — had been a respected member of the Free German Youth and had been a 'good' student at school. The newspaper asked why no one had reported the vandalism at the cemetery. The question, it seems, was purely rhetorical.

Finally there is the hardest question of all: that concerning the relationship between Nazism and Stalin. Until now, most East Germans have known unequivocally where they stood so far as Nazism was concerned. They have suppressed questions about Stalin's thinking in the later 1930s and in particular the peace agreement signed with Hitler in 1939 and Soviet behaviour after it was signed. 'Stalin,' said a Soviet magazine in October 1988, 'ordered the communist parties of the world to put an immediate end to anti-fascist propaganda . . .' Would there have been Hitler, the same magazine pointedly asked, without Stalin?

The magazine, called *Sputnik* and regularly used by East German schoolteachers to keep their pupils informed on Soviet developments under Gorbachev, was promptly banned. As for those who ordered the banning, some East German friends wondered, would they have been where they were today without Stalin?

It is in its perceptions of the wider world and in the formation of foreign policy that the thinking of the GDR leadership usually comes closest to the policies articulated from Moscow. In the European arena, almost all the polemics and the arguments have been directed towards the achievement and the maintenance of peace. Even the People's Army has been exhorted to exert greater efforts in the cause of peace. Individuals that one has met by chance at social occasions have said that their only concern was peace. Berlin in its 750th anniversary year (1987) was declared 'a city of peace'.

The ideal world, so far as opinion-formers in East Berlin are concerned, would dismantle tomorrow those security structures that may be considered as confrontational and would work instead towards what Gorbachev speech-writers might call 'a common security system' or 'a common European home'. Where is this détente leading to? one might ask. Well, comes the East German reply, perhaps to a way of finding the means to tackle together the economic, ecological and scientific challenges that have yet to be met.

The 'central issue of our time', according to Honecker, speaking at the end of 1988, was the 'safeguarding of international peace'. There had to be an end to the 'continuous squandering of enormous sums of money' on arms — a way of saying perhaps that defence bills placed a big strain on the economy — and instead a determination to spend this money on the 'social and cultural' needs of all nations, he said. He spoke of 'the peace programme of socialism' as though it were a well-read and familiar text to all who cared to hear.

None of these sentiments, give or take a few small nuances, would be out of place in other East European capitals. The GDR is without question an unflinchingly loyal member of the Warsaw Pact. It took part without hesitation in the Soviet-led invasion of Czechoslovakia in 1968, condemned the Solidarity trade unionists in Poland when they surfaced in 1981, and — here is a nuance — it closed ranks with President Nicolae Ceausescu of Romania, a fellow Pact member, when he was attracting the odium of much of the rest of the world for his human rights record.

Beyond Europe, East Germans maintain strong links with what they call the 'emergent nations'. It is one of the SED's top priorities, on the international agenda, to show 'active anti-imperialist solidarity' with all people who are fighting for 'national and social' liberation. This solidarity, furthermore, has extended to backing for a wish to see 'a new international economic order', based on equality.

Measured in terms of trade, these links do not add up to a great deal — less than 5 per cent of the country's total trading turnover. On recent figures, the main commercial partners in the Third World seem to be Iraq, as well as Iran, Brazil, Egypt and India. Trade relations, announced *Neues Deutschland* in 1987, went hand in hand with 'technological co-operation, cadre training and advisory work'.

The advisory work, during the 1980s, has been especially vigorous in the military sphere, with military 'experts' from the

GDR operating in Algeria, Angola, Ethiopia, Mozambique, Southern Yemen, Syria and Zimbabwe. It is also believed that guerrillas operating for the African National Congress and the South West African People's Organisation have had instruction at one time or another in East Germany. Leaders of both the ANC and SWAPO have been received in East Berlin several times since 1980, and Honecker and some of his ministers have made extensive tours to Black Africa.

Two countries not in the Third World are regarded with special interest by the East German leadership. These are Britain and the US, both of which Honecker would like to visit in his official capacity. Having been received, since the mid-1980s, in France and Spain as well as in West Germany, this should not be too difficult to achieve. However, British and American attitudes towards East Germany as the GDR are still cautious. British and American attitudes to the West Germans are something different. It is unlikely they would spit in the eye of a West German notion of a unified Germany. Honecker will have to wait a good deal longer.

The image of the West that several East German publications like to enhance is one which highlights drugs, crime and unemployment. When the popular American singer Bruce Springsteen came to East Berlin in 1988, he was described in the media as the champion of the dying towns and the downtrodden workers of the United States — hardly the language or the message of détente. It is not the only area where the media personnel of Honecker and Gorbacheve seem to agree to differ: the emphasis in Moscow when a Western rock artist pays a visit is nowadays on the music and the art, less on the social conditions which may have given rise to that music.

The Wind from Moscow

For understandable reasons, East Germany's relationship with the Soviet Union has become a very complicated dance in which each side is uncertain of the other's footwork. Since the troublesome Ulbricht was dispensed with in 1971, it has not always been clear who precisely was calling the tune.

Christian Morgenstern, the German poet and essayist, died in 1914. During his life he gained for himself one of a number of small niches in the German book of quotations for saying that while Russians love life as it is, Germans prefer it as it should be, could be and must be. Within a few years of his death, the Russians had turned their life upside down and the Germans had tried to do the same with theirs. But from the perspective of the late twentieth century, his view retains a curious validity. Life in the GDR today under the benevolently despotic SED is about how life should be, could be, must be.

When the Russians came to end the war in the spring of 1945 they had their own, often hate-filled, reservations about the Germans. Hitler's army had blasted its way across Soviet soil in 1941 and 1942 and the humiliations which were now to be inflicted on the Germans as a consequence can be understood. How many lurid tales could those old ladies in Berlin, on both sides of the Wall, tell if they wanted to? And how much anger, at the scale of the enforced reparations — which, according to Western estimates, amounted to $13 billion to the Russians alone — must still be smouldering in some German minds? It was a time when almost no German was in a position to argue.

When the Russians came again a little over forty years later, in a phalanx under party leader Gorbachev, the tune was entirely different. On that occasion, Gorbachev announced that the Soviet Union had just entered the state of developed socialism. Among those in the SED who listened to him were many who were convinced the GDR had entered that state long ago, possibly as much as twenty years earlier. When I watched Gorbachev as he went on a limited walkabout in East Berlin, close to the Schauspielhaus, on that April evening, the applause from the onlookers was polite, even warm in places, but it was not effusive.

Of course, friendship with the Soviet Union is writ large in all appropriate GDR pronouncements. Soviet policies are an important ingredient in the formulation of the GDR's foreign policy, to the extent that East Germans do much to promote Soviet disarmament interests in Europe and to train pro-Soviet armies in the Third World. The Soviet leader is the most honoured visitor when he comes to Berlin, but he knows as soon as he arrives that whatever control he may seek to exercise over his hosts, he has also to acknowledge their peculiarly East German determination to stand up for themselves.

A bi-lateral Treaty of Friendship, Co-operation and Mutual Assistance, binding on both signatories until the year 2000, has brought a formal closeness between the two sides. Although the Soviet partner, at the original signing in 1975, was Leonid Brezhnev, it has been to the advantage of his several successors that the GDR has since emerged as probably the best advertisement for a political economy under socialism. It has also proved to be a highly valued trading partner, and, for most of the time, an important ideological supporter. The People's Army is probably the best equipped in the entire Warsaw Pact, though whether all East German conscripts serve the Soviet Union and the Pact with undiluted enthusiasm must be open to doubt. (But then, conscripts everywhere have a rather jaundiced view of their 'duties'.)

Until 1979, there were an estimated 400,000 Soviet troops stationed on East German soil — a force twice as big as the East Germans' own. Occasionally, and especially in the garrison towns, they are visible but not obtrusive, though there have been occasional tales of rape, hooliganism and drunkenness. Otherwise, they rarely mix with local Germans except on public occasions. On the thirtieth anniversary of the GDR, Soviet ground forces were cut by 20,000 men and 1000 tanks. Further cuts were announced at the end of 1988 and in early 1989, also accompanied by the heavily publicised dismantling of some Soviet nuclear missiles. On these occasions, there was noise from the East German propaganda machine but no display of emotion. In 1983, when these missiles were first deployed, East German emotions had been distinctly mixed and by no means all positive.

Philosophically, the biggest problem arising for successive Soviet leaders in dealing with their East German counterparts is that the latter have consciously turned away from 'the Soviet model' in shaping political and economic policies. Instead, rather a deliberately 'GDR way' of doing things has taken shape, built on a sort of national pride, determination and discipline. This has meant that the GDR, in Honecker's words, has watched Soviet reforms in the late 1980s with 'much sympathy and great interest'.

There was thus more than a hint of patronage in the greetings conveyed to Moscow in November 1987, on the seventieth anniversary of the revolution. Congratulations, said Honecker and Stoph in a joint letter to Gorbachev, on your country's 'further advance on the road to socialism'. Who, it may be wondered, was patting whom on the back? Perhaps Gorbachev was avoiding unpalatable home truths when he encouraged other socialist countries to follow their own 'roads'. After all, they were almost all following their own 'roads' already.

At the end of 1988 this process reached a new phase, when the distribution of the Soviet magazine *Sputnik*, circulated to at least half a million readers in the GDR, was suddenly halted. It was read by many who followed closely but quietly the progress of the Gorbachev reforms. Now, it was suggesting that Germany's Communists, as well as the disruptive Stalin, may have been responsible for the advance of Hitler.

The stopping of the magazine was one of Honecker's more controversial public acts. It was an act of pride which betrayed a certain vulnerability. It led, so I was reliably told, to frenetic debates among party members, and even led to some of them resigning in protest. This was because, in spite of the almost pathological antipathy that some Germans still feel for Russians, there was also a large sector of the SED which wanted — by 1988 — to see Honecker undertaking some fundamental restructuring and reorientation of GDR policies along something like Gorbachev's lines.

When GDR historians using Moscow sources were able to disclose and discuss in some detail at the end of 1988 the fact that Stalin had liquidated large numbers of German Communists in the late 1930s, and had imprisoned others immediately after the Second World War, it was this same sector which offered most applause. I had a very searching conversation on this subject with a Humboldt University teacher, but Honecker, on this issue, said little.

Objective facts, as they say in East Berlin, state that Erich Honecker was born in 1912, that he will be replaced sooner rather than later, and that he will be succeeded by someone with probably very different priorities. Equally objective facts — though not everyone in East Berlin would agree — are that Honecker's leadership has indeed had its controversial aspects, that his attitudes to Gorbachev and the Gorbachev philosophy have indeed been the subject of fierce debate, and that many personalities in the highest echelons of power have been there too long for the country's good and are no longer able to motivate others with new ideas.

The GDR has had only two leaders in its first forty years — two men who may have had common experiences and common objectives but who were confronted by totally different times. The GDR after nearly twenty years of Honecker is not the country left by Walter Ulbricht. Preoccupations, expectations and geo-political realities have all changed. The global landscape, politically speaking, has changed as well, and so have East-West relations and German-German relations from what they were in 1971.

The pace is if anything increasing. Europe, East and West, is continually evolving, if Gorbachev and others have their way, towards a common European home, and if the GDR is to be part of that entity, it will have to evolve still further. In the last two decades, while the countries round the GDR, also calling themselves socialist and sitting in the same multinational forums, have altered, and sometimes very radically, the GDR has moved relatively little. In the 1980s, and approaching the 1990s, that has been the price of stability.

Honecker arrived at the party leadership less than halfway through the Soviet era of Leonid Brezhnev, the so-called 'period of stagnation' (not a phrase used by GDR publicists). The Soviet leadership has been replaced three times since then — its membership is almost unrecognisable — and the Communist movement has changed as a result. The GDR leadership has gone its own way.

This, of course, has not been how Honecker sees things. Socialism, he said in early 1989, was not 'static and unchanging'; new challenges had to be confronted, and each country had to confront them in a way appropriate to its own conditions.

'Today in the GDR,' said Joachim Herrmann, a senior politburo member, at about the same time, 'we foster the traditions of Karl Liebknecht, Rosa Luxemburg and their comrades-in-arms by turning a truly revolutionary programme into reality. We act in a revolutionary spirit.'

It was seventy years since the murder of the two revolutionaries whom he named. An estimated 250,000 Berliners were drafted in to hear him speak at the Socialists' Memorial Cemetery in Berlin's Friedrichsfelde. His words were comfortingly familiar to many who listened; to others, depressingly so. An unknown number of SED members positively ache to move forward.

An interesting talking point in the country in the last few years has been on 'the freedom to think differently' (a freedom which was pinpointed by Rosa Luxemburg). The answer to questions implicitly raised by this point is that the 'freedom' for such people is not necessarily the freedom which the GDR establishment wants to protect and guarantee. 'One must constantly check,' wrote one Professor Heinz Kamnitzer in *Neues Deutschland* in February 1988, 'for what and against what it is directed in order to decide who has the right to claim it as their own.'

Talk like this acknowledges there are gaps between the rulers and the ruled. The trouble is that so many gaps may be created as to leave the leadership more or less isolated, even from some of its supposedly strongest supporters. One friend, a lecturer in politics, has been an SED member for thirty years. He cares deeply about life in general and Socialism in particular, and his palpable honesty would probably delight the Gorbachev Kremlin. But he has been troubled by his work, he says, because it is a constant uphill struggle.

'We proclaim the GDR to be an oasis of peace, truth and achievement,' he told me, 'but it isn't quite like that. We are constantly told by our media that everything, or nearly everything, is fine, but Western television channels and dozens of Western radio stations which everyone can hear, tell a very different story. There are people in power who are terrified of glasnost.'

Keeping Soviet influences at arm's length has also meant keeping what Gorbachev calls democratisation at arm's length. There has been no public debate, nor even a public suggestion, as there has been elsewhere in Eastern Europe, that referenda should be held on issues of popular concern, that parliamentary and even party elections should be open to more than just centrally approved candidates, that independent trade unions should perhaps be countenanced, and the nomenklatura system of internal appointments based on party loyalty should be overhauled.

Gorbachev's published messages to Honecker have always had their positive side. In Moscow, in September 1988, he told Honecker and other East German visitors that 'thousands of threads, political, economic and ideological' bound the Soviet Union and the GDR. This speech by Gorbachev was not truncated when it appeared in the East German press, as others have been. The House of Soviet Science in East Berlin is regularly bombarded with requests for the products of glasnost.

The succession to Honecker has been a clouded area throughout his leadership. Two possible contenders, Paul Verner and Konrad Naumann, were removed from within notional striking distance in the mid-1980s. A third, Werner Felfe, who seemed to be in the Gorbachev reformist mould, died in 1988.

Others thought likely in 1989 to succeed include Egon Krenz, whose career pattern has been broadly similar to that of Honecker himself; Günter Schabowski, whose career was in journalism before he took over the Berlin SED machine; and Hans Modrow, a social scientist and career party man who now runs the SED in Dresden.

Any, or none, of these three could follow Honecker if he died soon, with the successor voted into place by the party politburo. How the succession will be achieved, if Honecker does not die soon, is not yet clear. There has only been one precedent.

Fifth Excursion: Honecker Comes West

When Erich Honecker, the man who supervised the building of the Berlin Wall, finally reached the Federal Republic in the autumn of 1987, the visit had been talked about in political and journalistic circles for three or four years, off and on. Differences between Bonn and Washington had been momentarily resolved, and Moscow had come to terms with East Berlin.

There were posters of Honecker, when he got there, on all the lamp-posts. They had been put up by the minuscule West German Communist party and gave the areas he was visiting the faintly exciting atmosphere of a by-election in a country constituency.

They depicted Dr Honecker, smiling and leaning forward like a solicitous and friendly general practitioner. He would solve your problems, they implied. Underneath was the proclamation that there should never again be war from German soil.

When he reached Trier, he came to the sort of city that Leipzig would like to be. It has a number of picturesque and historic buildings and is a bustling, apparently hard-working city, one of the oldest in Germany. It is not on everybody's tourist route but it is a place where people like to linger and savour its pleasantness. There are steamer trips on the Moselle, and there are wine-tastings. There are Roman remains and the market place provides as nice an urban environment as any in Germany in which to pause for a cup of coffee or a glass of local wine.

As he approached the birthplace of Karl Marx, it was the Junge Union — youth section — of the Christian Democrats who made the running in formulating greetings. A group of them, with banners and placards, were in the old Corn Market, near the post

178

office, protesting noisily and vehemently against the existence of the Wall. Some passing Communists were shouting back. Meanwhile a third group across the market place campaigned quietly for more German–German student exchanges.

Marx's birthplace is a solid bourgeois house in Brückenstrasse. Interestingly, it was acquired during the Weimar years by the Social Democrats, to be turned into a Marx museum back in 1928, but the inhospitable political climate meant the museum's opening had to be postponed. Finally, the Nazis took it over themselves and used it as a propaganda and printing base. After the war it was returned to the SPD, and on the centenary of Marx's death in 1983 it was re-opened, with an extension housing a library and research centre, as a museum. It stands just a few hundred yards from the spot in the market place where a street musician plays his accordion and a street artist offers his pavement rendering of Jesus Christ in chalk. Honecker, walking past these people in procession to the house, chatted to the local politicians who accompanied him. Occasionally, he waved, smiling, to bystanders and people looking out of upstairs windows who caught his eye. He took no notice of the younger elements from the CDU.

Inside the Marx house, badly in need of a fresh coat of paint, the distinguished visitor, whose whole political career has been conditioned by Marx's thoughts, placed a bunch of red roses. As he did so he heard the rhythmic chants of 'Murderer, murderer' from a group which had stationed itself just across the narrow street. They were out of sight, behind the official bus, but clearly audible.

Honecker still waved and smiled when he came out, but his proximity this time to the protesters meant that confrontation was in the air. At Müller's, the hairdresser, and Kolz, the tobacconist, situated on either side of the Marx dwelling, there must have been great sighs of relief when the man himself and the crowds he had occasioned had gone.

Two days before, history had been made when Honecker reached Bonn, where he had been welcomed with as much ceremonial and fanfare as he could wish. He was received by the Federal President and had what both sides agreed were 'frank and businesslike' talks with Chancellor Helmut Kohl. Agreements were signed to work together on environmental questions, on radiation protection and in specific areas of science and technology.

The sombre communiqué issued after the visit showed that long-standing preoccupations of the East German leadership had been acknowledged. Communists on both sides were doubtless well pleased.

The communiqué also talked about 'a commitment to understanding' and 'a sense of reality' and said these were to be the criteria for constructive co-operation between the two states. The loaded phraseology was welcomed by pragmatists on both sides. The note in the final paragraph that the Chancellor had accepted 'with gratitude' an invitation to come to the GDR 'in due course' was welcomed by more East Germans than West Germans. The latter group was made happy by Chancellor Kohl's reiteration before such a sensitive audience of his 'commitment' to 'the unity and freedom of Germany in free self-determination'.

Honecker had heard all this before, but never at a state banquet given in his honour in the West German capital. Perhaps Kohl thought he had scored a valuable point. But if he scored one, Honecker went on to score a few himself a day or two later when he went on to Neunkirchen, the old steel town in the Saar where he was born two years before the outbreak of the First World War. In that part of Germany, the posters of the genial GP were out in abundance.

Honecker took in an hour or two with his sister, who was still living in the locality. He also had a few minutes at the family grave, where the resting place of Familie Wilhelm Honecker is beneath a very simple marble slab between the Kohler and the Schenk families. Finally he met members of the brass band with whom he, as a more than passable drummer, had played in his youth. This particular reunion took place in the early evening and the warmth of it was enough to touch the hearts of the hardest member of the ultra-Conservative Christian Social Union. It did not matter, said some local people, that Honecker was not being made an honorary citizen. What mattered was that he was still an honorary member of the band. After all, they said, he was visiting home, wasn't he?

SELECT BIBLIOGRAPHY

Abrasimov, Pyotr. West Berlin: Yesterday and Today. Dresden, 1981.

Ardagh, John. Germany and the Germans. London, 1987.

Bahro, Rudolf. The Alternative in Eastern Europe. London, 1978.

Baylis, Thomas. The Technical Intelligentsia and the East German Elite. Los Angeles, 1974.

Botting, Douglas. In the Ruins of the Reich. London, 1985.

Brandt, Willy. People and Politics. London, 1978.

Bullock, Alan. Hitler: A Study in Tyranny. London, 1954.

Carr, William. A History of Germany, 1815–1949. London, 1979.

Carver, Terrell. Engels. Oxford, 1981.

Childs, David. Marx and the Marxists. London, 1973.

Childs, David. The GDR : Moscow's German Ally. London, 1983.

Chuikov, Vassily. The End of the Third Reich. London, 1978.

DDR Handbuch, Band 1 and 2. Bonn, 1985.

Deutscher, Isaac. Stalin: A Political Biography. Oxford, 1949.

Dokumente zur Geschichte der SED. Various editors. Berlin, from 1981.

Dominick, Raymond. Wilhelm Liebknecht and the Founding of the German Social Democratic Party. North Carolina, 1982.

Dorpalen, Andreas. German History in Marxist Perspective. Detroit, 1985.

Fletcher, Roger (editor). Bernstein to Brandt. London, 1987.

Dennis, Mike. German Democratic Republic. London, 1988.

Fischer, Ruth. Stalin and German Communism. Cambridge, Mass., 1948.

Fowkes, Ben. Communism in Germany under the Weimar Republic. London, 1984.

Gelb, Norman. The Berlin Wall. London, 1986.

Grebing, Helga. History of the German Labour Movement. London, 1969.

Gromyko, Andrei. Memories. London, 1989.

Grosser, Alfred. Germany in Our Time. London, 1971.

Harman, Chris. The Lost Revolution. London, 1982.

Harpprecht, Klaus. Willy Brandt: Portrait and Self-Portrait. London, 1972.

Herbst, Wolfgang (editor). Deutsche Geschichte, 1971–1945. Berlin, 1984.

Heym, Stefan. The King David Report. London, 1973.

Horstschanz, Günter, and Wimmer, Walter. Ernst Thälmann. Berlin, 1988.

Irving, David. The Destruction of Dresden. London, 1963.

Keiderling, Gerhard. Berlin 1945–1986. Berlin, 1987.

Keiderling, Gerhard, and Stulz, Percy. Berlin 1945–1968. Berlin, 1970.

Lange, Annemarie. Berlin in der Weimarer Republik. Berlin, 1987.

Lange, Annemarie. Berlin zur Zeit Bebels und Bismarcks. Berlin, 1984.

Leonhard, Wolfgang. Child of the Revolution. London, 1979.

Leonhardt, Rudolf. This Germany. London, 1961.

McCauley, Martin. The German Democratic Republic since 1945. London, 1983.

Mann, Golo. The History of Germany since 1789. London, 1968.

Merson, Allan. Communist Resistance in Nazi Germany. London, 1985.

Miller, Susanne, and Potthoff, Heinrich. A History of German Social Democracy. Leamington Spa. 1986.

Moreton, Edwina (editor). Germany between East and West. London, 1987.

Nettl, Peter. Rosa Luxemburg. Oxford, 1966.

A.J. Nicholls. Weimar and the Rise of Hitler. London, 1968.

Prol, P.P. Germany: Unification to Weimar. Edinburgh, 1982.

Raddatz, Fritz (editor). Marx — Engels: Selected Letters. London, 1981.

Scharf, C. Bradley. Politics and Change in East Germany. Colorado, 1984.

Scheele, Godfrey. The Weimar Republic: Overture to the Third Reich. London, 1946.

Schwarz, Helga. Karl Liebknecht: Krieg dem Kriege. Berlin, 1986.

Shukman, Harold (editor). The Blackwell Encyclopedia of the Russian Revolution. Oxford, 1988.

Simmons, Michael. Berlin: The Dispossessed City. London, 1988.

Stahl, Walter (editor). The Politics of Postwar Germany. New York, 1963.

Steele, Jonathan. Inside East Germany. London, 1977.

Stolper, Wolfgang. The Structure of the East German Economy. Harvard, 1960.

Taylor, A.J.P. (editor). The Communist Manifesto. London, 1967.

Trotsky, Leon. The Struggle Against Fascism in Germany. New York, 1971.

Ulbricht, Walter. Whither Germany? Dresden, 1966.

Waller, Michael, and Fennema, Meindert (editors). Communist Parties in Western Europe. Oxford, 1988.

Wilson, Edmund. To the Finland Station. London, 1942.

Wolfe, Bertram (editor). Rosa Luxemburg: The Russian Revolution. Michigan, 1961.

Wolff, Theodor. Through Two Decades. London, 1936.

In addition to this list, there are scores of guide books, handbooks, propaganda tracts and other bits and pieces picked up over the years from places visited, conferences attended, and from helpful individuals. They are too many, and in some cases too esoteric, to justify a separate list, but with this all-embracing paragraph, they are indeed acknowledged.

INDEX